*Empowered lives.
Resilient nations.*

ASSESSMENT OF DEVELOPMENT RESULTS
EVALUATION OF UNDP CONTRIBUTION **PACIFIC ISLAND COUNTRIES**

Evaluation Office, February 2012
United Nations Development Programme

REPORTS PUBLISHED UNDER THE ADR SERIES

Afghanistan	Colombia	Jordan	Serbia
Argentina	Republic of the Congo	Lao PDR	Seychelles
Bangladesh	Ecuador	Malawi	Somalia
Barbados and OECS	Egypt	Maldives	Sudan
Benin	El Salvador	Mongolia	Syrian Arab Republic
Bhutan	Ethiopia	Montenegro	Tajikistan
Bosnia and Herzegovina	Georgia	Mozambique	Thailand
Botswana	Ghana	Nicaragua	Turkey
Brazil	Guatemala	Nigeria	Uganda
Bulgaria	Guyana	Papua New Guinea	Ukraine
Burkina Faso	Honduras	Peru	Uzbekistan
Cambodia	India	The Philippines	Vietnam
Chile	Indonesia	Rwanda	Yemen
China	Jamaica	Senegal	Zambia

ASSESSMENT OF DEVELOPMENT RESULTS: EVALUATION OF UNDP CONTRIBUTION – PACIFIC ISLAND COUNTRIES

Copyright © UNDP 2012, all rights reserved.
Manufactured in the United States of America. Printed on recycled paper.

The analysis and recommendations of this report do not necessarily reflect the views of the United Nations Development Programme, its Executive Board or the United Nations Member States. This is an independent publication by the UNDP Evaluation Office.

Editing: Sanjay Upadhya
Graphic design: Suazion, Inc. (NY, suazion.com)
Cover photos provided by UNDP Fiji

ACKNOWLEDGEMENTS

This evaluation could not have been completed without the contributions from many people. Our thanks are extended to stakeholders and partners of UNDP Multi-Country Offices in Fiji and Samoa and the Pacific Centre, including members of the governments of the Pacific Island Countries, civil society, international development community, the United Nations family and members of the islands that the evaluation team visited during the course of the exercise.

The Evaluation Office would like to express its gratitude to the members of the national reference group for their valuable contribution in revising the terms of reference and draft reports. The reference group was comprised of Elizabeth Koteka, Director, Central Policy Planning Office, Office of the Prime Minister; Pasha Carruthers, National Environment Service; and Jim Armistead, Aid Management Division in the Cook Islands. In the Federated States of Micronesia, Jackson Soram, Multilateral Desk Officer, Department of Foreign Affairs. In Fiji, Pita Wise, Permanent Secretary for Strategic Planning, National Development and Statistics; Filimone Waqabaca, Permanent Secretary, Local Government, Urban Development, Housing and Environment; and Lorraine Seeto, Advisor to the Governors, Reserve Bank of Fiji. In Kiribati, Terieta Mwemwenikeaki, Deputy Secretary, Ministry of Foreign Affairs; Kurinati Robuti, Senior Economist, Ministry of Finance and Economic Development; Boorau Koina, Accountant and Administrator of Kiribati Integrated Framework for Trade, Ministry of Commerce, Industry and Cooperatives; and Ribeta Abeta, Senior Environment Inspector, Ministry of Environment, Lands and Agricultural Development. In Nauru, Taiatu Ataata, Deputy Secretary of Finance; and Klenny Harris, Department of Foreign Affairs. In Niue, Jay Gataua, Acting Head of Office for External Affairs. In Palau, Gustav N. Aitaro, Director, Bureau of International Trade and Technical Assistance. In the Republic of the Marshall Islands, Bernard Adiniwin, Assistant Secretary for Multilateral Affairs, Ministry of Foreign Affairs. In Samoa, Noumea Simi, ACEO Aid Coordination, Ministry of Finance; Roina Vavatau, SUNGO; Nynette Sass, CEO Chamber of Commerce; Sooalo Mene, Parliamentarian; Palanitina Toelupe, Health Sector representative; and Sharon Aiafi, Foreign Affairs representative. In the Solomon Islands, Channel Iroi, Under Secretary Technical, Ministry of Environment, Climate Change, Disaster Management and Meteorology; and Gane Simbe, Deputy Governor, Reserve Bank of Solomon Islands. In Tokelau, Jovelisi Suveinakama, Director, Office of Tokelau, Apia; and Ake Puka-Mauga, Office of Tokelau, Apia. In Tonga, Mahe Tupouniua, Secretary for Foreign Affairs, Ministry of Foreign Affairs; and Natalia Palu, Acting Deputy Secretary for Aid Management Unit, Ministry of Finance and National Planning. In Tuvalu, Tupagao Falefou, Permanent Secretary for Foreign Affairs, Ministry of Foreign Affairs; Teniku Talesi, Assistant Secretary for Home Affairs and Rural Development; Letasi Lulai, Director, Planning and Budget; and Lopati Samasoni, Director, Rural Development. In Vanuatu, Peter Tari, Deputy Governor of the Reserve Bank of Vanuatu; Collin Tavi, Head of the Monitoring and Evaluation Unit, Prime Minister's Office; and Johnny Koanapo, Head of the United Nations Division, Department of Foreign Affairs.

The evaluation would not have been possible without the commitment demonstrated by Knut Ostby and Nileema Noble, UN Resident Coordinators and UNDP Resident Representatives in Fiji and Samoa respectively, Garry Wiseman, the director of the UNDP Pacific Centre in Suva, and the able contribution of Toily Kurbanov, Deputy Resident Representative in Fiji and Armstrong Alexis, Coordinator for Programme and Operations in Samoa. We very much appreciate the cooperation received from Asenaca Ravuvu and Mereseini Bower, Ronald Kumar, Margaret Sapolu and Georgina Bonin and the programme and project staff of UNDP in Suva and Apia. We would also like to thank the UNDP Regional Bureau for Asia and the Pacific, in particular, Sitara Syed and Vineet Bhatia for their comments and valuable support and contribution to the ADR process.

The UNDP Evaluation Office would like to offer its sincere thanks to the evaluation team. The team was ably led by Mohamed Nurul Alam and comprised Tupeni Baba, Kolone Vaai and Gabriela Byron. Thanks also go to Oscar A. Garcia, the UNDP Evaluation Office task manager, who also prepared the evaluation design. Elizabeth de Leon Jones provided valuable research support. The Evaluation Office would like to thank the entire evaluation team for their dedication and hard work throughout the exercise.

The quality enhancement and administrative support provided by Evaluation Office colleagues is critical to the successful conduct of all evaluations. The report benefited from reviews also from Vijayalakshmi Vadivelu and from comments made by Masahiro Igarashi who participated in the stakeholder meeting held in Nadi, Fiji. Many thanks are due Sonam Choetsho and Thuy Hang Ti To who provided valuable management and administrative support to the evaluation process. Marina Blinova and Anish Pradhan assisted in the editing and publication process with the external help of Sanjay Upadhya.

FOREWORD

This is the report of the first independent country-level evaluation conducted by the Evaluation Office of the United Nations Development Programme in the Pacific Island Countries (PICs). The ADR Pacific is distinctive in terms of its multi-country dimension and spatial spread. The evaluation examines UNDP contributions to the development results in 14 PICs scattered all over the Pacific Ocean. UNDP had two multi-country programmes managed by two Multi-Country Offices in Fiji and Samoa. The ADR reviewed the period from 2002 to 2011, which includes the previous and the ongoing UNDP country programmes (2003–2007 and 2008–2012). The evaluation has two main components: analysis of UNDP's contribution to development results through its programme outcomes, and the strategy and positioning it has taken in support of those interventions. The evaluation aims to present recommendations as inputs for adjustments to current strategies and for future programming.

The evaluation found that UNDP's programme focus on poverty reduction and the achievement of the Millennium Development Goals is of immediate strategic relevance to the needs of the PICs. Pacific island governments have recognized poverty as a concept relevant to the Pacific that needs to be addressed through pro-poor policies and good governance, as the region continues to live through the adverse impact of the global economic and financial crises.

It is well known that policy and institutional weaknesses are at the heart of constraints to growth and poverty reduction in the Pacific. Good governance is central to achieving the development goals pursued by the PICs. UNDP programmes in specific countries concentrated in supporting strengthening and reforming parliaments, constitutional reform, civic education and broader support to local governance and decentralization.

The focus of the governance area on strengthening of parliaments, and constitutional and electoral reforms are considered highly relevant in nation building as the predominantly traditional social and political structures are being moulded into centralized national government structures.

UNDP responsiveness in times of natural disasters and emergencies was widely appreciated by the governments, the donors and affected communities, particularly in managing post-disaster responses in Samoa, Tonga, Cook Island and Solomon Islands. UNDP's prompt response in emergencies was effective and well coordinated with all UN resources available in the region.

Sustainable development becomes an intense challenge in the face of acute increasing environmental risks and degradation. Population growth, urbanization, and an increased demand for cash income contribute to the emergence of localized environmental and natural resource management concerns. Climate change is a significant Pacific concern of global origin. UNDP's sustained support in the mainstreaming of environment and climate change issues in national development strategies has been instrumental in generating policy-level attention on environmental issues in the PICs. However, the results in supporting national capacity assessment and capacity development for environment management in compliance with the international conventions are variable.

Efficiency of programme management by UNDP over the two programmme cycles has been mixed. Programmatic efficiency in terms of appropriate design, targeting stakeholders, distribution of focus and activities between upstream and downstream level were considered moderately satisfactory. The main issue of concern was managerial efficiency involving timeliness of approval of projects, timely procurement of inputs, and recruitment of technical experts/consultants, disbursement of funds.

The evaluation has provided a number of recommendations to allow UNDP to build on the lessons learned from its programme in the past years. UNDP's emphasis of work at central and policy level should be balanced with opportunities for work at downstream and outreach level with civil society organizations and communities in view of good experiences of effectiveness observed during the current cycle. Downstream work should be used to inform policy-making.

The evaluation recommends adopting a differentiated programme strategy and approach for smaller island countries due to their specific situation, high unit cost of delivery and inherent capacity constraints. The development needs and interventions in the region should be assessed based on the nature of the country.

UNDP's comparative advantage as a repository of global knowledge and experience requires more application at programme and project level. This would also enhance the quality of project-level development work.

The evaluation team made an effort to reflect in the report the specific development challenges faced by each country and identify streams of future cooperation based on lessons learned from past experience. I hope the results of the evaluation will be useful to strengthen the partnership between UNDP and the Pacific island countries in the achievement of sustainable development results.

Juha I. Uitto
Deputy Director, Evaluation Office

CONTENTS

Acronyms and Abbreviations ix

Executive Summary xi

Chapter 1. Introduction 1
    1.1 Objective and Scope 1
    1.2 Evaluation Framework 1
    1.3 Evaluation Methodology 2
    1.4 Analytical Framework 4
    1.5 Process 4
    1.6 Limitations 5
    1.7 Structure of the Report 6

Chapter 2. Subregional Development Context 7
    2.1 Geographical and Demographic Background 7
    2.2 Recent Economic Trends in the Pacific 8
    2.3 Equitable Economic Growth and Poverty Reduction 10
    2.4 MDGs and Human Development 11
    2.5 Governance 13
    2.6 Environment, Climate Change and Disaster 14
    2.7 Peace and Stability 16
    2.8 Gender Equality 17
    2.9 Development Cooperation and Aid Effectiveness 18

Chapter 3. The United Nations and UNDP in the Pacific 21
    3.1 UNDP Overview and Structure 21
    3.2 UN Development Assessment Framework 22
    3.3 UNDP Multi-Country Programmes 23
    3.4 UNDP Results and Resources Framework 25

Chapter 4. Contribution of UNDP to Development Results 31
    4.1 Outcome 1. Poverty Reduction and the Millennium Development Goals 31
    4.2 Outcome 2. Governance and Human Rights 39
    4.3 Outcome 3. Crisis Prevention and Recovery 48
    4.4 Outcome 4. Environment and Sustainable Management 51

Chapter 5. Strategic Positioning   **63**

    5.1 Strategic Relevance and Responsiveness   63
    5.2 Comparative Strength   64
    5.3 Partnership   64
    5.4 Contribution to UN Values and Cross-cutting Issues   68
    5.5 MCO Management Issues   74

Chapter 6. Conclusions and Recommendations   **77**

    6.1 Conclusions   77
    6.2 Recommendations   81

Annexes   **83**

    Annex 1. Terms of Reference   83
    Annex 2. Evaluation Matrix   95
    Annex 3. Sample of Projects   99
    Annex 4. People Consulted   101
    Annex 5. Documents Consulted   111

Figures

    Figure 1. Analytical Process   5
    Figure 2. Samoa MCO Delivery   26
    Figure 3. Fiji MCO Delivery   26
    Figure 4. Pacific Centre Delivery   27
    Figure 5. Consolidated Expenditure of Fiji and Samoa MCOs (2004-2010)   28

Tables

    Table 1. Evaluation Criteria   2
    Table 2. Overview of Data Collection Methods and Sources   4
    Table 3. Key Economic Indicators   9
    Table 4. Human Development Index and Human Poverty Index Values (1998 and 2008)   12
    Table 5. Official Development Assistance for Pacific Island Countries
                and Aid Flows by Donors (2009)   20
    Table 6. Consolidated Expenditure of Fiji and Samoa MCOs (2004-2010)   28
    Table 7. Programme Budget and Expenditure by Fiji MCO (2004-2010)   29
    Table 8. Programme Budget and Expenditure by Samoa MCO (2004-2010)   29

ACRONYMS AND ABBREVIATIONS

ADB	Asian Development Bank
AusAID	Australian Agency for International Development
CCA	Common Country Assessment
CDM	Country Development Manager
CEDAW	Convention on the Elimination of All forms of Discrimination against Women
CSO	Civil Society Organization
CPD	Country Programme Document
CPAP	Country Programme Action Plan
CRC	Convention of the Rights of the Child
CROP	Council of Regional Organizations of the Pacific
EC	European Commission
EEZ	Exclusive Economic Zone
EU	European Union
FAO	Food and Agriculture Organization
FFA	Forum Fisheries Agency
FSM	Federated States of Micronesia
HDI	Human Development Index
HIES	Household Income and Expenditure Survey
HOPS	Heads of Planning and Statistics (Pacific)
HPI	Human Poverty Index
HRBA	Human Rights Based Approaches
IATF	Inter-Agency Task Force
ILO	International Labour Organization
JPO	Joint Presence Office
JSM	Joint Strategy Meeting
KDP	Kiribati Development Plan
LDC	Least Developed Country
MCPD	Multi-Country Programme Document
MCO	Multi-Country Office
MDGs	Millennium Development Goals
MDG-TF	Millennium Development Goal Trust Fund
MOE	Ministry of Education
MSI	Mauritius Strategy for Implementation
MTP	Medium Term Plan
MTR	Mid-Term Review
MTSP	Medium Term Strategic Plan
NDP	National Development Plan

NGO	Non-Governmental Organization
NHRI	National Human Rights Institution
NPC	National Planning Commission
NRA	Non-Resident Agencies
NZAID	New Zealand Aid for International Development
OCHA	Office for the Coordination of Humanitarian Affairs
ODA	Official Development Assistance
OHCHR	Office of the High Commissioner for Human Rights
PAA	Vanuatu National Development Strategy
PICs	Pacific Island Countries
PIFS	Pacific Islands Forum Secretariat
ROAR	Results Oriented Annual Report
RBM	Results-based Management
RC	Resident Coordinator
RCO	Resident Coordinator's Office
RCM	Regional Coordination Mechanism
RMI	Republic of the Marshall Islands
SIDS	Small Island Developing States
SOPAC	Pacific Islands Applied Geo-science Commission
SPBEA	South Pacific Board for Educational Assessment
SPC	Secretariat of the Pacific Community
SPREP	Secretariat of the Pacific Regional Environment Programme
TCPR	Triennial Comprehensive Policy Review
UNAIDS	UN Joint Programme on HIV/AIDs
UNCAC	UN Convention Against Corruption
UNDAC	United Nations Disaster Assessment and Coordination
UNDAF	United Nations Development Assistance Framework
UNDG	United Nations Development Group
UNDP	United Nations Development Programme
UNESCAP	United Nations Economic and Social Commission for Asia and the Pacific
UNESCO	United Nations Educational, Scientific and Cultural Organization
UNFCC	United Nations Framework Convention on Climate Change
UNFPA	United Nations Population Fund
UNHCR	United Nations High Commissioner for Refugees
UNICEF	United Nations Children's Fund
UNIFEM	United Nations Development Fund for Women
UNISDR	United Nations International Strategy for Disaster Reduction
USP	University of the South Pacific
WFP	World Food Programme
WHO	World Health Organization

EXECUTIVE SUMMARY

The Assessment of Development Results (ADR) in the Pacific is an independent evaluation conducted in 2011 by the United Nations Development Programme (UNDP) Evaluation Office. The objective of the ADR Pacific is to assess UNDP's contributions to development results in the Pacific subregion and how the organization has positioned itself to support and add value to the development efforts of the Pacific Island Countries (PICs). It was timed to be conducted in 2011 so that its findings and conclusions can inform the process of formulation of the new multi-country programmes in the Pacific beginning in 2013.

The ADR Pacific is distinctive in terms of its multi-country dimension and spatial spread. It covered 14 PICs scattered all over the Pacific Ocean spanning about six thousand miles from the east to the west. The two multi-country programmes are managed by two Multi-Country Offices. The ADR reviewed the period from 2002 to 2011, which includes the previous and the ongoing UNDP country programmes (2003–2007 and 2008–2012). The evaluation has two main components: analysis of UNDP's contribution to development results through its programme outcomes, and the strategy and positioning it has taken in support of those interventions. Following the standardized methodology for ADRs, the evaluation assessed results in all four key outcome areas of poverty reduction, governance and human rights, crisis prevention and recovery, and environment and sustainable development. Two important cross-cutting issues addressed in the evaluation included gender equality and capacity development perspectives in UNDP programmes.

The ADR applied the criteria of strategic relevance, effectiveness, efficiency, sustainability, and promotion of United Nations values A larger evaluation framework (matrix) was developed by the evaluation team linking each of the criterion and sub-criteria with related specific questions, data sources and data collection methods. The ADR required the synthesis of findings to be pitched at a higher strategic level with an analysis of credible links between UNDP efforts and national development results. Hence, it was also important to ensure that the higher level analysis is grounded in country-based project-level evidence and findings and, at the same time, the methodology accommodates questions ranging from macro-level country policies to examining project-level micro results.

The specific steps in the ADR process included: background research, two country visits for evaluation scoping and for data gathering, report writing and quality assurance. Prior to finalization, the Governments of the 14 PICs, UNDP Multi-Country Offices in Fiji and Samoa and the Regional Bureau for Asia and the Pacific reviewed the ADR. The review process also benefitted from a stakeholder meeting in October 2011.

MAIN FINDINGS: CONTRIBUTION TO DEVELOPMENT RESULTS

POVERTY REDUCTION AND THE MDGS

UNDP's programme focus on poverty reduction and MDGs is of immediate strategic relevance to the needs of the PICs. Poverty has emerged as a significant and growing issue for most PICs. The national statistics display growing disparities in income, opportunities and well-being between rural and urban dwellers, and a growing underclass of landless, urban poor. Inability on the part of Pacific island economies to generate enough formal and informal sector jobs and livelihood opportunities has been contributing to the rise in poverty and income inequality as well as to 'poverty of opportunity'. As such, Pacific Island governments have recognized poverty as a concept relevant to the Pacific that needs to be addressed through pro-poor policies and good governance. The Pacific subregion also continues to live through the adverse impact of the global economic and financial crises. This has reversed or slowed down progress in many countries. Recognizing that MDG framework would be the most useful vehicle in focusing and improving the integration of policy, planning and budgeting into national sustainable development strategies, all Pacific countries have committed themselves to achieve the MDGs and have taken ownership by internalizing or localizing the MDGs.

In this context, UNDP's focus on poverty and supporting national efforts of achieving the MDGs is highly relevant, timely and proving to be effective in facilitating national efforts. The activities under this outcome include a substantial number of project and non-project initiatives of UNDP systematically targeting integration of poverty in national development planning, developing poverty strategy and mainstreaming MDGs in the national context, sectoral plans and budgeting; generating accurate macro-economic and poverty data for pro-poor policy analysis; costing sectoral priorities.

Specific MDG and poverty-related support was provided to Samoa, Vanuatu, Kiribati, Solomon Islands, Tonga, Cook Islands, Nauru, Fiji and Tokelau, Palau and Marshall Islands. The interventions were generally focused more at policy and strategy level. The project interventions supported evidence-based policy formulation and institutional strengthening. In many countries, the project processes and outputs contributed to changes in mindset and perceptions of policy-makers (Samoa, Vanuatu, Palau). There was tangible progress observed in the capacity of planning and statistical institutions at the central level.

GOVERNANCE AND HUMAN RIGHTS

It is well known that policy and institutional weaknesses are at the heart of constraints to growth and poverty reduction in the Pacific. All the countries assessed have adopted the Pacific Plan objectives of "improved transparency, accountability, efficiency in management and use of resources in the Pacific". The PICs aim to achieve sustainable and equitable economic growth and poverty reduction in the medium term. Good robust governance is central to achieving the MDGs being pursued by the PICs.

UNDP interventions in specific countries through the country programme since 2004-2011 concentrated in supporting, strengthening and reforming parliaments, constitutional reform, civic education and broader support to local governance and decentralization through enhancing community participation, capacities of outer island communities, facilitating service delivery, developing and supporting institutional framework for decentralized governance. UNDP programmes included initiatives and projects to support national policy capacities and governance systems to exercise the principles of inclusive, equitable, participatory, transparent and accountable governance and respect for human rights.

The focus of the governance thematic area on strengthening of parliaments, and constitutional and electoral reforms are considered highly relevant in these relatively new independent countries, as the predominantly communal-based traditional social and political structures are being moulded into centralized national government structures. Ownership of governance reforms at the national and community levels appear more pronounced for the relatively small island states as shown in the cases of Cook Islands, Tokelau and Nauru. The support to decentralization and local governance is serving this aspiration through extensive project work at subnational levels and outer islands.

Effectiveness of the governance component on supporting the Pacific Islands Forum Principles of Good Leadership and Accountability, which was targeted mainly through the strengthening of parliaments, has been rated relatively successful, as highlighted by the results of the parliamentary strengthening projects in Solomon Islands,

Kiribati, Nauru and Marshall Islands. Effectiveness of the component on enhanced decentralization of governance and participatory decision-making has been limited. This is due to the relatively more complicated designs of these types of projects for widely scattered and often geographically isolated islands/communities, which need relatively long period of implementation to get some traction, as shown in the cases of Cook Islands, Kiribati, Solomon Islands, Cook Islands and Vanuatu. Effectiveness of UNDP in advocating anti-corruption practices has picked up in the last 12 months with the accession of Vanuatu in July 2011 to the UN Convention against Corruption (UNCAC). Since then, a number of other Pacific countries (Tuvalu and Solomon Islands) have started to take action towards acceding to UNCAC.

In both streams of governance projects (Strengthening Parliament and Support to Decentralization), there was evidence of efforts by governments in allocating human resources and institutional support (Vanuatu, Solomon Islands, Kiribati). However, the scale of support in some instances was not adequate. The long-term sustainability is ensured when outputs are internalized within national systems. In the parliament projects, that was generally visible. But in the other areas such as decentralization, it is too early to judge, although there was evidence of strong government support, budgetary outlay and institutional structure (Solomon Islands, Kiribati) which are essential preconditions of long-term sustainability. More positive outcome of these projects was observed in relatively smaller island states, where there was closer involvement of communities. The civic education projects involving non-government and community-based organizations, interest groups and public school systems provide good model for mainstreaming civic concepts as important ingredient for building conscious citizenry.

CRISIS PREVENTION AND RECOVERY

UNDP assistance in this area was aimed at strengthening the capacity of PICs to prevent and manage crises and build resilience to the impact of tensions and disasters. Exposure to natural hazards such as volcanoes, tsunamis, cyclones, earthquakes (Solomon Islands and Vanuatu are among the most disaster-prone countries in the world) and experiences of civil unrest and conflict over the past decade (Fiji, Solomon Islands, Tonga and Vanuatu), have highlighted the need to focus more strongly on disaster risk reduction, peace and stability dialogues, early warning systems, and the role of women in crisis prevention and recovery. In the long term, it is increasingly recognized that democratic governance and poverty reduction are key in preventing potential conflicts.

Under this outcome, UNDP focused on formalizing institutional mechanisms for mainstreaming disaster risk reduction into national development and budgetary strategies (in Solomon Islands and Vanuatu); and development and implementation of national policies and plans addressing human security through conflict-sensitive analysis and tension-reduction interventions (in Fiji, Marshall Islands, Tonga and Solomon Islands). This outcome was supported through projects providing (a) support to the development of an integrated approach to addressing and reducing vulnerability to tension and disaster; (b) effective recovery strategies that seek to build capacity to address the root causes of humanitarian crisis and natural disasters; and (c) addressing the long-term livelihood needs of communities.

UNDP's best responsiveness has been demonstrated in times of natural disasters and emergencies. UNDP role in promptly responding and managing post-disaster response in Samoa, Tonga, Cook Islands and Solomon Islands were widely appreciated by the governments, the donors and affected communities. Countries accorded high satisfaction with UNDP's prompt response in emergencies coordinated with all UN resources available in the region (Cook Islands, Tonga, Samoa, Solomon Islands). However, less effort was visible in advocating and supporting development of institutional mechanism for disaster response system nationally. This area has a strong potential for UNDP involvement with long-term essential capacity development for the PICs.

ENVIRONMENT AND SUSTAINABLE MANAGEMENT

Heavy reliance on fragile land and in-shore marine environments characterize the Pacific economies and livelihoods. Sustainable development becomes an intense challenge in the face of acute increasing environmental risks and degradation. Population growth, urbanization, and an increased demand for cash income contribute to the emergence of localized environmental and natural resource management concerns. Climate change is a significant Pacific concern of global origin.

UNDP support in this arena is considered most relevant and timely. The support was provided through three streams of efforts: a) strengthened national capacity to develop and implement environmental policies, legislative and management frameworks and mainstreaming through national policies and budgets; b) strengthened capacities for improved access and management of multilateral environmental agreements; c) sustainable livelihoods of vulnerable groups strengthened through institutional support and leveraging indigenous governance systems, to contribute to sustainable environmental management.

UNDP's sustained support in mainstreaming of environment and climate change issues in national development strategies has been instrumental in generating policy-level attention on environmental issues in PICs. This resulted in efforts for developing institutions and impetus in formulating national policy and institutional framework in environment. Institutional and technical capacity of the environment staff within the governments has improved (Fiji, Samoa, SOI, Vanuatu, and Kiribati) over the years as reflected in their better management of environmental issues within their respective countries. However, there is variability in such capacities among the countries. In the area of national capacity assessment and capacity building for environment management in compliance with international conventions, the UNDP interventions supported national efforts, which heightened awareness and generated required national processes reasonably effectively.

GENDER EQUALITY

The ADR found a number of good gender-specific, or women's empowerment projects operating at the regional level. For example, connected with the programme to support Parliament is a very high-profile effort to promote temporary special measures to increase women's representation in Parliament, and in some cases excellent empowerment and advocacy through mock Women's Parliaments.

At the MCO and national levels, progress on gender has been slow and varied across countries and projects depending more on the capacity and outlook of the individuals involved than on a common UNDP understanding. Gender is interpreted quite differently across the staff and partners and given different weight in programme planning. The most consistent and positive results have been achieved in the area of the MDGs which, to varying degrees, have improved the incorporation and analysis of disaggregated data. This represents potential for improving gender equality since it collects and monitors data on gender issues, as well as sex-disaggregated data on a range of issues that can then be analysed with a gender perspective. As it is incorporated into national systems, this information should be useful for a range of policy decisions.

At the MCO levels, both offices developed gender strategies in 2007-2008. These strategies represent an important step in promoting and mainstreaming gender equality. However, results are still few. At the project level, there is little analysis. Even in cases where it was specified as a project output – such as the Sustainable Land Management projects in seven of the Fiji MCO countries, and the Community Centred Sustainable Development Projects in the four Samoa MCO countries – it has not been done.

CAPACITY DEVELOPMENT

The UNDP Country Programme Action Plans generally stress the importance of capacity building at the national level. Generally, capacity development is considered an essential underpinning of UNDP activities, UNDP programming guidelines emphasizes application of a comprehensive framework for capacity development in programme and project formulation. The UNDP analytical framework for capacity development consists of a three-tier strategy consisting of higher enabling policy environment for capacity development, institutional capacity at different levels in public sector (and civil societies) and individual capacity development at the base through education, training and empowerment. Most UNDP projects tend to have capacity development intent, sometimes pronounced and other times implied. In spite of the importance of this aspect of programming, there is no overall analysis or strategy outlining the approaches to capacity development in the context of the Pacific. Very few projects also had any capacity assessment as part of the formulation.

There are some good examples of successful capacity building. The Parliamentary Support project in Solomon Islands, for example, shows the value of a multifaceted systemic approach to capacity development. In a number of cases (Samoa, Cook Islands, Vanuatu) there has been a significant improvement in national capacity to collect data at all levels, analyse it, select appropriate indicators to measure progress (especially relating to MDGs) and incorporate the findings into new national development strategies. In Cook Islands, Samoa, Niue, Nauru, Vanuatu and Tonga national capacities have been improved to assess climate vulnerabilities, generate climate scenarios and make policy decisions for appropriate mitigation and adaptation measures. Samoa MCO's support through South-South Cooperation and Capacity Development Projects (SSCCDPs) over the past two decades has clearly been useful for government capacity development through access to training, professional development and support of consultants.

CONCLUSIONS

Conclusion 1: Development Results

Overall UNDP in the Pacific has made important contributions during the period under review to meet the development challenges that the countries are facing. Good inroads have been made in mainstreaming and internalizing MDGs in the planning and budgetary processes of the countries. Substantial progress has been achieved in understanding poverty as a pressing development issue through policy and analytical research. Progress is also notable in some spheres of democratic governance. There is good achievement in the area of crisis prevention and recovery in terms of responding to immediate disaster and strengthening disaster management. Innovative and downstream approaches have shown good results in the area of energy and environment. Efforts and important national initiatives were supported in the area of gender equality with mixed success. Finally, capacity development was a built-in and cross-cutting strategy in project and programme interventions. The contribution in this sphere remains fraught with endemic challenges of brain drain, rotation within public service and out-migration. In many cases where the expected results have not been met or their achievements are delayed, this has been largely due to a combination of factors including those outside UNDP's control. With this qualification, UNDP has been generally effective in its contributions to the subregion.

Conclusion 2: Relevance

The four areas of outcome focus continue to be most relevant for the medium term with additional complementarities with downstream interventions and dispersal of efforts to subnational, outer islands or depressed areas. UNDP interventions during the two programme periods addressed a development agenda relevant to all PICs through an overarching strategic programme focus as a basis for individual country projects and initiatives. The programmes spanned from responding to most urgent challenges of disasters to supporting various spheres of longer term goals of democratic governance; from responding to macro issues of national poverty to provision of solar energy to households; from forging partnership with key national government agencies to regional organizations and bilateral donors to working hand in hand with downstream civil society organizations on local development initiatives. Operating effectively within this wide range of spheres and partners, UNDP demonstrated its ability for consistent strategic alignment of its activities, to be imaginative and responsive, and its agility of operating within a dynamic partnership environment.

To ensure better relevance and effectiveness, UNDP based on experience should consider differentiated strategy for interventions in smaller island countries (called micro states). Experience in the region has shown that relevance of the standard approach which has worked for most of the Pacific island countries is limited in the context of the so called micro states. The development needs of these countries require attention at downstream and local-level interventions. Service provision in micro states is always more costly and effort-intensive because of their thin government structures and lack of critical mass of trained people due to brain drain.

Conclusion 3: Effectiveness

Development results of UNDP interventions show a wide variance in terms of effectiveness. They varied from country to country, by areas of focus, by level of national preparedness, by level of resource and by degree of partnership with stakeholders. The projects were generally well designed in a consultative way, but often suffered from delays in approval and start-up process. The responsibility for this is shared by both the national and the UNDP side. Implementation delays are a normal phenomenon in the Pacific with delays or inability in designating technical counterparts, in consultant recruitment process and erratic flow of required budget resource from UNDP's side. Many times, projects operate in a stand-alone existence outside the mainstream action or institutional structure of the government agency/ministry, which makes its eventual integration difficult.

Effectiveness in terms of progress towards outputs has been generally satisfactory and at times excellent, but progress towards outcome is more varied and difficult to ascertain. It was difficult to establish a proportionate link among the hierarchy of outcome statements in reference documents like the UNDAF, the MCPD, the CPAP and the project documents. Effectiveness in actualizing results has been much greater where the projects were driven by the government agency's priority and integrated within its current plan.

Overall, the attention to project-level technical monitoring and enhancing easy access by projects to UNDP's technical knowledge and support still remains an urgent necessity. Better acceptance and consideration of policy-level work by the government can be facilitated by technical quality assurance of processes and outputs by technically competent professionals. Project outputs with policy implications also require a momentum of substantive deliberation overtime with different levels in government. This requires qualified and articulate professionals in the subject area to be available periodically at the project level.

Conclusion 4: Efficiency

Efficiency of programme management by UNDP over the two programme cycles has been mixed. Programmatic efficiency in terms of appropriate design, targeting stakeholders, distribution of focus and activities between upstream and downstream level, managing stakeholders, etc., were considered moderately satisfactory with some exceptions. Overambitious plans and unpredictable sources of funding at times caused initiatives to stall and face inefficiency.

The main issue of concern was managerial efficiency involving timeliness of approval of projects, timely procurement of inputs, and recruitment of technical experts/consultants, disbursement of funds. The perceptions from majority of the countries and counterparts were negative. Although fund disbursal has improved significantly over the years, the perception of inefficiencies remains. The approval of management and financial issues from the two MCOs for outlying country projects was mostly considered slow or sluggish. UNDP's procedures, regulations, paper trail, and reporting requirements are not always understood at project level. The geographical coverage and challenges of administering programmes in remote countries and locations, and the centralized nature of UNDP MCO administrations, leave the project offices with limited authority of resource allocations, recruitment and procurement. Sometimes weak competence of national project staff, staff turnover at national level and lack of handing-over procedures also contribute to delays and inefficiencies.

Efficiency of project management at the site level, especially at sub-national or outer island level, was weak. Late designation of counterparts, high turnover, lack of proper understanding of processes, lack of substance on the project are some of the chronic problems. Proper and regular monitoring and follow-up by UNDP could be instrumental in detecting and solving some of these issues. Some projects pointed out lack of creative solutions and inability to adapt to unanticipated changes by the project personnel also creates delays. However, high operational costs (travel, communications, etc.) limits UNDP monitoring to one per year (Northern Pacific) and twice, resources permitting, for most nearby countries – specifically for project management and monitoring.

There were also endemic rigidities in the national execution and national implementation processes which may have been the cause of some delays. For the PICs, the amenability of applying NEX or NIM should be assessed carefully, considering the capacity constraints and based on criteria of efficiency, transaction costs and cost in terms implementation delays due to inadequate response capacity of the government apparatus. This issue requires to be raised at the headquarters policy level for requesting flexibility in specific cases.

High turnover in UNDP staff in the Samoa MCO and the sub-office in Solomon Islands is seen as limiting effectiveness and efficiency of projects, resulting in a negative image of organizational effectiveness. The frequent and sizeable staff turnover was pointed out as problematic by counterparts. This phenomenon not only delays but also at times interrupts smooth project implementation due to lack of or delayed action from UNDP. Stability in human resource is a sine qua non of good performance. While there may be valid reasons for such turnover, this issue needs to be analysed by UNDP to come up with some pragmatic and systemic solutions for the longer run.

The UN Joint Presence Offices have been applauded by the governments and they are already showing effectiveness. They are seen by the countries as facilitators of troubleshooting, communications with the MCOs and logistics management for projects and missions by UN agencies. Their capacities may be leveraged even more in the future for programme support functions.

Conclusion 5: Sustainability

Greater sustainability was observed in projects that supported initiatives with strong national ownership and commitment backed by established national strategy and budgetary allocation. For example, UNDP support of the MDG process and its integration in national policy and planning enjoyed significant promise of longer sustainability. At the project level, sustainability has been affected by lack of attention to institutional integration, lack of adequate capacity development and preplanning of exit and sometimes external factors.

Positive experiences and potential of sustainability emerged in projects where there was close engagement with CSOs in managing resources and processes. This was backed by commitment to sustain the project benefits by local population groups. When downstream service-oriented projects or sustainable resource management projects are eventually handed over to CSOs or local institutions, they usually survive the test of time. The experiences have been solidified through CCSDP and SGP projects which had very strong CSO, NGO and popular interface. These experiences should be codified for use in the forthcoming programme cycle.

Capacity development goes beyond technical training and imparting skills to people. A systemic view and institutional approach helps better to ingrain capacities within the institution. An example of good practice is support to parliaments. These initiatives took a systemic view of work streams in parliament and tried to enhance the capacities in various ways, i.e., training, handbooks, and establishment of committee structure, record management systems and procedures. It proved to be effective and sustainable.

Different layers of institutions require a mix of support such as short-term technical interventions, and long-term in situ technical capacity development. Given the focus of UNDP on reforms, it should consider longer term sustained support to those initiatives. One-off support to a longer term issue remains a tendency of UNDP.

Conclusion 6: Comparative Strength

UNDP leverage as a repository of global knowledge and development experience and a gateway to global network is underutilized. The opportunity is missed to leverage the joint strength of the MCOs and the Pacific Centre in a systematic and synchronized way to deliver best knowledge, capacity and technical substance at the country level. The intrinsic perceptive divide and lack of integrated management structure is identified as the main reason for less than optimal performance in this area.

UNDP's substantive niche and capacity to deliver is well recognized in policy-oriented poverty work, governance, crisis prevention and recovery. UNDP strength and knowledge for technical GEF project formulation and project management expertise is generally acknowledged by the governments and other stakeholders. In view of the increasing number of agencies with more technical clout crowding the area, UNDP needs to establish a specific niche for itself (beyond competence in project management support) in the area of environmental governance. This role will enable it to retain its role as one of the main development agencies in environment.

Conclusion 7: Promotion of UN values

The performance is satisfactory in terms of promotion of UN values. MDGs and poverty analysis work had good effect in the mindset of policy-makers in a number of countries. However, work on gender equality and human rights-based approaches require more attention and follow through at project level work. Capacity for gender analysis and integration of gender dimension require attention in-house and should be a dimension in performance management system. At a macro level, capacity development would be greatly enhanced by an overall country- or ministry-level strategy for capacity development, to enhance the potential for interventions to contribute to national priorities. That can be supplemented by a practical strategy for capacity assessment and development at project formulation stage and monitoring during implementation.

Conclusion 8: Partnership and coordination

UNDP has maintained a good level of positive and useful partnership across the governments, donors, regional organizations and civil society organizations. The new frontier of partnership with CSOs in downstream work in civic education, environment, sustainable livelihood and development, and decentralization needs to be leveraged for greater results at the local level. The partnership for work with the regional organizations requires a coordinated strategy with other UN system organizations in the Pacific. Instead of a perception (which may be mutual) of competing in some areas, the strategy should focus on leveraging comparative and value-added strength of UNDP in promoting effectiveness and sustainability of national programmes.

The work in UN coordination seemed to be effective with an excellent interactive and willing environment. The UNDAF framework has given a window of opportunity to bring the UN system's strength to support development in the Pacific. But not much work was evident in promoting the effort in joint programming or integrated country-oriented programming, an area which should be a natural next step for the UN system.

RECOMMENDATIONS

Recommendation 1: Programme focus

The four outcome areas with gender equality as a cross-cutting theme continue to be most relevant for the PICs. Hence, emphasis for the next programme cycle should be continued and consolidated in those areas. Experiences on some of those areas have started generating nationally embedded endeavours. Policy analysis and programme intervention support in the areas of poverty, employment, sustainable livelihood, food security, governance (parliament, electoral assistance, civic education, and decentralization), private sector, environment and climate change, and crisis prevention should continue to receive priority attention.

Recommendation 2: Programme strategy

UNDP's emphasis of work at central and policy level should be balanced with opportunities for work at downstream and outreach level with CSOs and communities in view of good experiences of effectiveness and results observed during the current cycle. This is particularly suitable in smaller islands. Downstream work should be used to inform policy-making.

A differentiated programme strategy and approach could be considered for smaller island countries due to their specific situation, high unit cost of delivery and inherent capacity constraints. The development needs and interventions should be assessed based on the nature of the country. For example, options could be pursued for fewer and more integrated projects to reduce management workload, special measures for meeting capacity gaps, and joint/shared programme frameworks with other agencies.

A coherent strategy should be strengthened and implemented for mainstreaming of gender equality. It should include a shared gender analysis at the regional level and at the national level. The analyses should assess priorities and opportunities for promoting gender equality and/or women's empowerment that should inform UNDP strategy. The project formulations must include a gender analysis for use in project management. Programme staff should have access to support and resources in this regard.

The capacity development intent and content of projects should be made explicit at formulation stage with a detailed capacity assessment and statement of a strategy for capacity development which should be monitored and accounted for in progress reports.

Recommendation 3: Project cycle management

UNDP should accord priority and adequate technical support to this aspect. Project formulation should be addressed in a technically competent fashion. A thorough appraisal of the government's priority, and the project's embeddedness in institutional context and capacity, should be undertaken during formulation to include all aspects.

Country demand management for substantive and technical support: Introduce a regime of organized country demand management in programming with a tight management oversight to address issues emerging at country project level and time-bound response system. UNDP should intensify conducting regular project management monitoring of progress. More importantly, it should introduce technical monitoring through quality-assurance support of important products of the projects. The difference between the two types of monitoring should be understood clearly. Technical professionals' services should be drawn from the Pacific Centre, if available, or from outside if necessary for this purpose. Monitoring should identify areas or products which require higher level dialogue and engagement within the government and policy-makers. This continued engagement with professional inputs is essential to ensure effectiveness of project outputs.

Monitoring and evaluation: Introduce a more thorough and disciplined monitoring and evaluation system as part of wider management

strategy. A system of holding agenda-based periodic tripartite review meetings could be introduced coinciding with monitoring visits to countries/projects. Monitoring of activity schedules, outputs, progress towards outcomes and project/programme finances should be carried out and recorded as part of an institutional system. This documented information is essential as a base for monitoring and evaluation. Project and outcome evaluations should be planned, monitored and carried out with due diligence with clear accountability assigned to programme staff and management.

Recommendation 4 : Efficiency

Efficiency issues should be addressed on a number of fronts:

1. **Choice of implementation mode should be guided by the country situation rather than the corporate prescription of UNDP.** The feasibility and efficiency of working with NEX and DEX modality should be studied in each case to choose the appropriate modality. If required, a well-argued case for flexibility in small islands should be made by the MCO to UNDP Headquarters based on efficiency and results considerations. Reasons should be identified for the trend in delays in approvals. If some systemic and process prescriptions require more time, provide it in the planning phase and avoid unrealistic planning targets at the outset.

2. **More flexible HR modalities or options for project-level recruitment should be introduced.** Introduce retainer contracts, periodic technical support from institutions in the region, where recruitment of longer term technical personnel is proving difficult.

3. **The issue of delays in fund transfers to projects should be addressed.** The system of transfer should work with equal efficiency in all cases, unless there are explainable constraints. At the project level, appropriate training should be imparted in cash-flow planning and management.

Recommendation 5

Production of a periodic subregional Human Development Report should be considered to facilitate advocacy work on sensitive issues in the subregion and also to provide added support for promotion and compliance with UN values.

Recommendation 6

Connect, integrate, and infuse UNDP's global knowledge and solution to Pacific project-level work. The Pacific Centre's comparative advantage in terms of its current work, focus and proven knowledge management competence should be coordinated with the MCOs' country demand management system. UNDP's comparative advantage as a repository of global knowledge and experience requires greater application at the programme and project levels. This would also enhance the quality of project-level development work. This requires systematic and intentionality in application.

Recommendation 7

Introduce an institutional oversight system which would enable the MCOs and the Pacific Centre to consolidate the organization's strength to deliver better-quality development assistance. The performance of the current rules of engagement should be reviewed and applied with regular oversight by the senior management of the MCOs and the Pacific Centre. A **dedicated participatory management deliberation between the MCOs, the Pacific Centre and Regional Bureau for Asia and the Pacific is recommended** to seriously explore potential options and follow it up with bold decisions to implement all consequential changes such as integrated work plan, clear decision-making structure and accountability and financial management. If the distinctive UNDP aspect of global knowledge infusion in programmes is not made visible and useful, its position as a value-adding partner to the PICs may be undermined.

Chapter 1

INTRODUCTION

1.1 OBJECTIVE AND SCOPE

The Evaluation Office (EO) of the United Nations Development Programme (UNDP) conducted an Assessment of Development Results in the Pacific Island Countries (ADR Pacific) in 2011. ADRs are conducted to capture and demonstrate evaluative evidence of UNDP's contributions to development results at the country level, as well as the effectiveness of UNDP's strategy in facilitating and leveraging national effort for achieving development goals. ADRs are carried out within the overall provisions contained in the UNDP Evaluation Policy,[1] following the methodology developed by EO for ADRs.

The purpose of an ADR is to:

- Provide substantive support to the Administrator's accountability function in reporting to the Executive Board
- Support greater UNDP accountability to national stakeholders and partners in the programme countries
- Serve as a means of quality assurance for UNDP interventions at the country level
- Contribute to learning at corporate, regional and country levels

The objective of the ADR Pacific was to assess UNDP's contributions to development results made during the current and previous programme cycles 2003-2007 and 2008-2012, in 14 Pacific Island Countries (PICs)[2] delivered through the two Multi-Country Offices (MCO) in the region. It analysed how UNDP in the Pacific has positioned itself to support and add value to the efforts of the PICs to promote development of their countries and people. The ADR exercise generated conclusions and lessons learned with a view to contribute to the organization's future positioning in the Pacific subregion. It was conducted in 2011 to provide inputs to the preparation of new multi-country programmes beginning in 2013, which are to be approved by UNDP's Executive Board in 2012. With this purpose in perspective, the ADR also generated a set of recommendations for consideration to inform and support the process of deliberation and formulation of the country programmes.

1.2 EVALUATION FRAMEWORK

The evaluation was conducted keeping in context the national development objectives and priorities, and the goals of the Multi-Country Programme Documents (MCPD) which respond to current and emerging development challenges of PICs. The programmatic focus of UNDP Pacific is on four key inter-related outcome areas of poverty reduction, governance and human rights, crisis prevention and recovery, and environment and sustainable development.

The evaluation has two main components: i) analysis of the UNDP's contribution to development results through its programme outcomes, and ii) the strategy and positioning it has taken in support of those interventions. In assessing these two elements, the evaluation followed the

---

1   <www.undp.org/eo/documents/Evaluation-Policy.pdf>
2   Cook Islands, Federated States of Micronesia, Fiji, Republic of the Marshall Islands, Niue, Palau, Vanuatu, Tokelau, Tuvalu, Tonga, Kiribati, Nauru, Samoa and the Solomon Islands.

Table 1. Evaluation Criteria

Relevance: Extent to which an intervention addresses the development challenges of the country and supports the national development strategies and policies reflecting the needs of the Pacific Island countries.

Effectiveness: The extent to which planned results are being achieved, or likely to be achieved at the level of outcomes.

Efficiency: The relationship between outputs and inputs in terms of human and financial resources (costs) focus, timeliness, and management.

Sustainability: The extent to which the results and benefits of the assessed activities would continue or would be likely to continue, once initiatives are completed.

Promotion of UN Values: The extent of promotion and application of values of human rights and development, gender equality, advocacy for achieving MDGs and other international conventions.

'UNDP ADR Method Manual' which prescribes specific criteria elaborated below.

Analysis was carried out on the contribution of UNDP to development results in the PICs through its programme activities. The analysis is presented by thematic/programme areas and according to the following criteria: relevance; effectiveness; efficiency; and sustainability. The ADR addressed the extent to which the programme responded to conditions and features which are specific to Small Island Developing States (SIDs), especially in the areas of service delivery, strengthening of institutional capacity of the states (including clarifying the meaning of capacity development in the region) and issues relating to gender equality and women's empowerment, and climate change adaptation.

The positioning and strategies of UNDP are analysed both from the perspective of the organization's mandate and the development needs and priorities in the countries. This entails systematic analyses of UNDP's place and niche within the development and policy space in the Pacific, as well as strategies used by UNDP to maximize its contribution. The following criteria were applied: relevance and responsiveness; exploiting comparative strengths; and promoting UN values from human development perspective.

Within the analyses, wherever applicable and to the extent possible based on evidence, attention was paid to UNDP's effectiveness in promoting gender equality, capacity development, in leveraging partnerships for development, and coordination of UN and other development assistance. The ADR team adopted a flexible and, wherever necessary, a nuanced approach to application of the evaluation criteria and key questions.

The UNDP MCOs in the Pacific work as development partners of 14 different countries and territories spread over an enormous geographical expanse. This physical spread and the number of countries to be served from two locations add to operational complexities. For example, it has Joint Presence Offices which facilitate operations and coordination in specific countries. What are its implications for effectiveness and efficiency of programmes? Also, the presence of the UNDP Pacific Centre with a substantial regional programme has implications for coordination, complementarities and synergy for development results. The ADR considered selective aspects on management and operations to the extent they influenced the development results and strategic positioning.

1.3 EVALUATION METHODOLOGY

The Evaluation Matrix (Annex 2) was developed to link each of the criterion and related questions to data collection and the data sources. This was used by the evaluation team as the common reference document at all stages of the evaluation process.

ADR Pacific is based on qualitative data collection and analysis of primary and secondary sources.

Given the variety of countries covered and the time constraints, the data collection for Pacific ADR was quite a challenge. The team flexibly used multiple methods of data collection that included document reviews, workshops, group and individual interviews, project/field visits and surveys. In view of the diversity of country conditions and variability of quality and adequacy of data availability, the evaluators used the following two data collection methods at a minimum:

Document review was a principal source of data collection. The team reviewed national plans, political and development reports, budgets and sectoral reports related to UNDP programme, significant reports prepared by donors or regional organizations. Other important documents included all monitoring products, progress reports, documents produced as outputs, project evaluations, and sectoral/thematic evaluations. The team, in particular, reviewed whatever monitoring data was available in UNDP and project offices to assess performance under each of the outcomes of the country programme and any review reports related to projects and programmes.

Stakeholder interviews were another important mode of primary data collection. A strong participatory approach was taken involving a broad range of stakeholders including both insider (e.g., relevant beneficiary government officials, UNDP staff, project managers, technical advisers, other UN agency personnel) as well as those beyond UNDP direct partners (e.g., bilateral and multilateral donors, civil society organizations, private sector, project beneficiaries). The semi-structured interviews were conducted individually with key informants or in groups on selected topics, face to face, or by telephone. Field observations were collected by evaluators through visits and interviews at select project sites in each country. The projects for visits were selected beforehand based on the criteria of critical importance and accessibility.

1.3.1 DATA COLLECTION ON THEMATIC LEVEL: PROJECT-RELATED INFORMATION

Primary data was collected through individual interviews, field visits, and where possible focus groups. Telephone interviews and electronic survey were used wherever necessary and feasible. The evaluation team mapped 60 projects (Annex 3) for more intensive examination supported by UNDP during 2003-2011 distributed across the four results areas. For manageability of scale, it was necessary to reduce the sample size. Projects not covered by visits were covered through desk reviews. Project-level analysis was carried out based on monitoring data, reviews and evaluation studies. The sample size and list of projects was agreed upon based on coverage of outcome, volume of funding, balance between upstream and downstream initiatives and balance among countries.

The evaluators visited 11 out of the 14 countries and carried out data collection through interviews and, where possible, group interviews with key officials and counterparts in different countries. The purpose of the country visits was to collect information, data and, more importantly, obtaining first-hand perceptive observation on the nature of progress being made in outputs and outcome areas.

1.3.2 DATA COLLECTION ON UNDP STRATEGIC POSITION

Primary data on this dimension were collected through individual interviews and focus-group discussions. The stakeholders involved included UNDP, selected United Nations organizations, government institutions (particularly at the central level), bilateral and multilateral donors, civil society, and significant personalities considered conversant with Pacific development issues and country context.

Non-project activities: UNDP activities are not limited to projects. They also include other initiatives such as stakeholders' consultation, advocacy, networking, resource mobilization and

Table 2. Overview of Data Collection Methods and Sources		
Level	**Method of data collection**	**Sources**
Strategic level	Interviews (individual) Focus groups	UNDP, resident United Nations organizations, government institutions, bilateral and multilateral donors, civil society and sectoral specialists conversant with country context
Thematic/ Programmatic level: Project activities	Desk review	A select sample of projects (a total of 60 projects mapped between 2002 and 2010) were selected for in-depth desk review. The sample is representative of the main thematic areas and sub-areas in which UNDP is involved.
	Interviews and field visits	Interviews were conducted for the sampled projects in each country visited with project authorities, executing agencies and project users. The objective of the interviews was to collect as much primary information as possible and elicit perceptions from stakeholders that have been engaged at different stages and with different roles in UNDP interventions.

coordination. Primary data on this aspect was collected mainly through individual interviews and focus group discussions.

1.4 ANALYTICAL FRAMEWORK

The preparation of the final evaluation report had the challenging task of distilling an enormous volume of project-level data and evidence collected from 14 countries to a higher-level synthesis of key findings and conclusions. The evaluators had to exercise professional discretion, and a disciplined approach without compromising rigour in reducing the large volume of data gathered. Triangulation for validity of findings was carried out by comparing findings on same questions across different sources of evidence, across countries and across practice areas.

The final evaluation report format for the ADR requires synthesis of findings at a higher strategic level. This means that the content cannot be confined to project-level analysis and information, although a significant portion of the analysis has been grounded in country-based project-level evidence and findings. Hence, the important ingredients for higher synthesis were generated using the findings and evidence from the country reports prepared by the evaluators based on their visits. Unlike other (one country) ADRs, in this case the country reports by the evaluation team members provided the main core of evidence and ingredients for the final analysis and report writing. The format for generating project-level interviews and country report was collectively agreed upon by the evaluation team at the initiation workshop of the team in Fiji before the start of the country visits. The analytical process followed the steps depicted in Figure 1.

1.5 PROCESS

In view of the scope and multi-country approach, the evaluation had to be consultative and sensitive to the needs of the wide variety of stakeholders in all the countries. After the formulation of the terms of reference (TOR), a scoping mission to both the MCOs was carried out by the EO in May 2011. In consultation with the MCOs and the government, a National Reference Group was set up in all countries. The Reference Group was consulted on the finalization of the ToR and the inception report prepared by the evaluation team was also shared with the Reference Group well ahead of the start of the country visits.

The ADR Pacific was conducted by an independent evaluation team comprising of a team leader, three specialist members and a senior evaluator task manager from EO. The main evaluation mission was conducted for three weeks in August-September followed by an intensive

Figure 1. Analytical Process

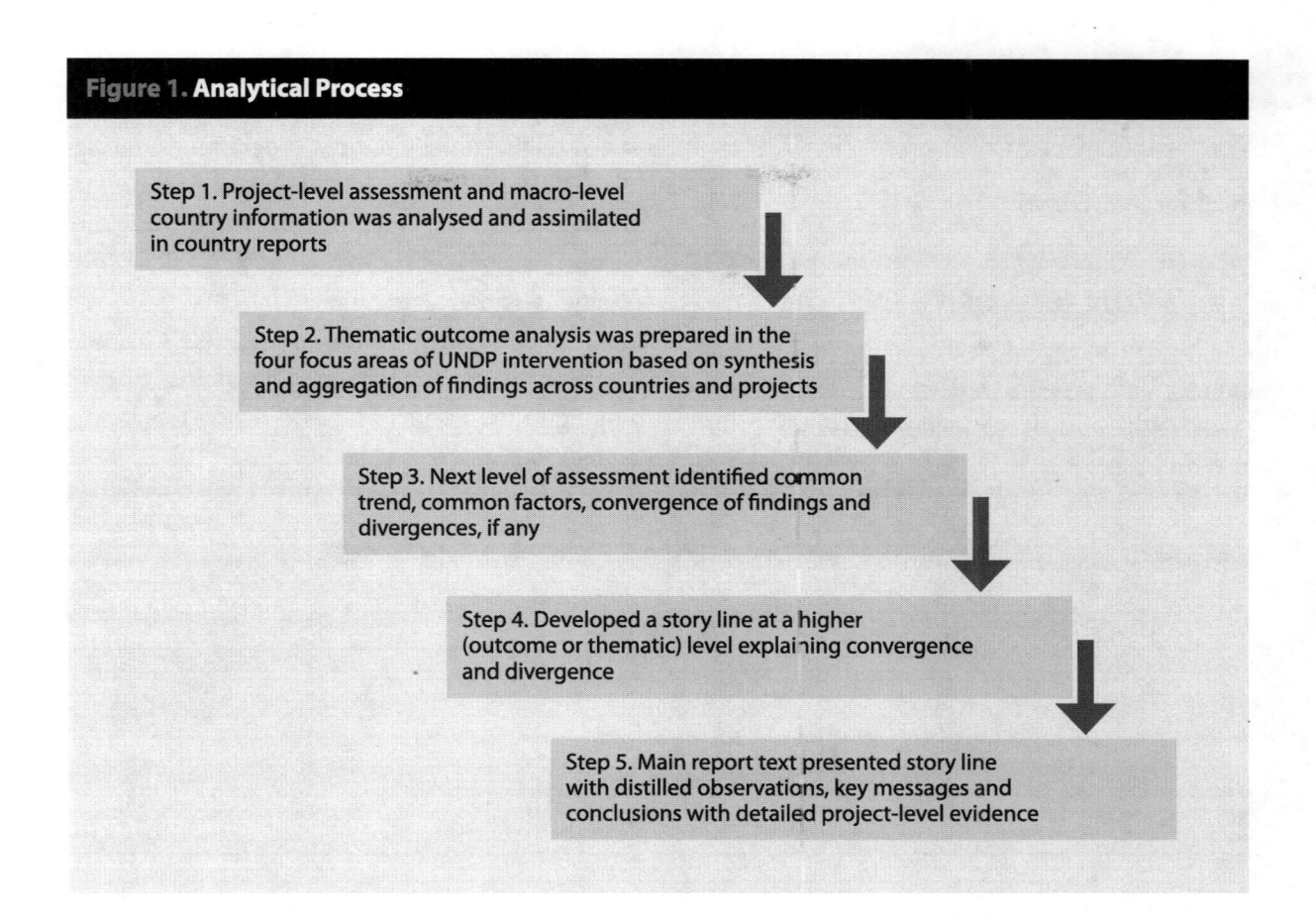

- **Step 1.** Project-level assessment and macro-level country information was analysed and assimilated in country reports
- **Step 2.** Thematic outcome analysis was prepared in the four focus areas of UNDP intervention based on synthesis and aggregation of findings across countries and projects
- **Step 3.** Next level of assessment identified common trend, common factors, convergence of findings and divergences, if any
- **Step 4.** Developed a story line at a higher (outcome or thematic) level explaining convergence and divergence
- **Step 5.** Main report text presented story line with distilled observations, key messages and conclusions with detailed project-level evidence

four-day data analysis by the team in Fiji. The first draft of the main report has undergone an EO quality assurance scrutiny, and was discussed at a wider stakeholder meeting in Fiji at the end of October 2011.

1.6 LIMITATIONS

The limitations faced by this evaluation are more than those associated with the usual one-country ADR. What differentiated it most from other ADRs was that data collection was divided geographically rather than thematically, so that as many countries as possible could be visited. Beyond this, the principal limitations have been the very short time span for in-country data collection, inadequacy of available information, absence of outcome data related to indicators, and weak baseline data in most cases. Project-level monitoring information such as periodic project reports, interim assessments, reports on visit were less than satisfactory across countries. In many cases, availability of key government counterparts for consultation left gaps in information. In some cases, site visits had to be cut short or missed due to time constraint. Limited time and accessibility permitted visit to only one small island country (Nauru) and the remaining three such countries (Tuvalu,[3] Tokelau and Niue) remained out of team's itinerary. Although considerable secondary documentations on those countries were analysed and telephone interviews conducted, visits certainly would have deepened the understanding of specific development issues in micro states. In spite of limitations, the evaluation team maximized the use of available

---

3 For example, a visit was planned to Tuvalu, but there were limited flights that were fully booked for the duration of the fieldwork.

CHAPTER 1: INTRODUCTION

information and data and best effort was made to maintain credibility of evidence, eliminate any possible bias and address the main evaluation questions based on evidence, introspection, triangulation, and analysis.

1.7 STRUCTURE OF THE REPORT

Chapter 2 provides the subregional development context and presents analytical information to contextualize the development needs and priorities of the PICs that serve as a basis for UNDP strategy. Chapter 3 provides a snapshot of the strategic orientation and programme content of the UNDP Multi-Country Programmes during the 2003-2007 and 2008-2012 programme periods, including the organizational structure of and financial information on UNDP in the Pacific. Chapter 4 examines UNDP's contribution to development results in the PICs. Chapter 5 extends the analysis to UNDPs strategic positioning in the Pacific. Finally, Chapter 6 presents conclusions and recommendations.

Chapter 2
SUBREGIONAL DEVELOPMENT CONTEXT

2.1 GEOGRAPHICAL AND DEMOGRAPHIC BACKGROUND

The Pacific Subregion, spanning approximately 6,000 miles across the Pacific Ocean from the east to west, is composed of 22 small island countries and territories, of which 14 are covered by UNDP programmes. The coverage excludes the American Samoa, French Polynesia, Guam, New Caledonia, Northern Mariana Islands, Pitcairn, and Wallis and Futuna. The countries and territories are also classified in three different clusters: Polynesia (Cook Islands, Niue, Samoa, Tokelau, Tonga, Tuvalu), Melanesia (Fiji, Solomon Islands, Vanuatu), and Micronesia (Kiribati, Marshall Islands, Nauru, F.S. Micronesia, Palau). The subregion is geographically vast and culturally and ecologically diverse. Each one of the countries/territories has its own character and particularities. They have varying land size, population, natural resource endowments, economy, income levels, cultures, physical attributes, colonial heritages, languages, degrees of social cohesion, and economic and social policies. While the region has a mix of middle income and Least Developed Countries (LDCs), it also reflects a wide variability in human development terms.

The islands are either high-volcanic mountainous or low-coral formations. Most of the land is at sea level but there are some volcanic chains in Vanuatu, Solomon Islands, Samoa, Palau, F.S. Micronesia, Fiji, and Cook Islands. None of the countries have common land borders. Most of these islands are not bigger than a few square kilometers. The four largest countries, Solomon Islands (28,370 sq km), Fiji (18,333 sq km), Vanuatu (12,190 sq km) and Samoa (2,935) occupy over 94 percent of the total land mass. The smallest, Tokelau is only 12 sq km.

The Pacific islands have a total population of 2.3 million, according to 2010 estimates.[4] In most countries, the male population is larger than the female, with the exception of Nauru. The region has high rates of population growth, and its young age structure (around one third of the islands' population are aged under fifteen years)[5] indicates that such trends will continue in the coming generations. Besides the age pyramid, the high fertility rates (average 4.5 births per woman in 2008)[6] and the low mortality indicators help to amplify the high population growth problem. This demographic boom and transition, high under-15 population, large number of births and increasing proportion of elderly population creates additional demand on health care, education, and social services. However, large overseas migration in some of the countries of the region has acted as a demographic safety valve causing a countervailing depopulation trend. Migration also has become the source of economic opportunities, and remittances. On the flip side, it has also been translated in a continuous negative 'brain drain' flow resulting in skills shortage in the home countries.

Most of the territories have a high density of population with related depletion of resources usually caused by this condition. This is the case of Nauru, Tuvalu, and Marshall Islands with

---

[4] Country sources, International Database (US Census Bureau 2010)

[5] House, W.J., 'The Role and Significance of Population Policies in the Pacific Islands', *Pacific Health Dialog*, Vol. 2. No. 1, Suva, 1995.

[6] United Nations, Department of Economic and Social Affairs, Population Division.

465, 433, and 299 people per square kilometre respectively. Some of the PICs are multi-island countries, with many of the islands being sparsely populated or uninhabited. Internal migration from outer islands to the centres is common in the region increasing the trend towards urbanization in many of the countries, causing an upward pressure on land, housing, water, sanitation, health and education services. However, the urban population is still lower than 50 percent of the total population.

2.2 RECENT ECONOMIC TRENDS IN THE PACIFIC

The PICs face a range of common development constraints in varying degrees, typical to small island nations. These include vast distances within and between them, and to world markets; small and dispersed local markets; and high unit costs of social and economic infrastructure provision. These factors of physical isolation, limited economies of scale, small populations, limited overland natural resources (in most cases), lack of infrastructure, adverse impact of climate change, natural disasters, and economic shocks all contribute to the vulnerability and fragility of the economic structure in most of the Pacific islands. However, PICs have substantial potential in mining of marine resources in the Exclusive Economic Zones (EEZs) and untapped seabed minerals. In addition, fertile land and favourable climates for agricultural production, attractive sites for tourism development and some natural resources (such as gold in Fiji and forests in the Solomon Islands) provide good potential for generating productive economic activities. On a more positive note, good potential exists for sustainable economic and social development in these countries. Widespread subsistence productions along with strong social support systems have helped prevent the occurrence of absolute poverty in the PICs.

The Pacific island economies continue to suffer from the adverse impacts of the global economic crises, although most PICs (except Fiji, Samoa and Tonga) registered positive GDP growth, with Solomon Islands and Vanuatu recovering faster than others. High energy and commodity prices continue to create inflationary pressure, which in turn tends to increase poverty levels, as real incomes decline throughout the region. The region as a whole faced an average estimated inflation rate of 5.4 percent in 2011.

The region is particularly susceptible to energy price movements because of distances between and within countries, and to the food crisis because of the high dependence in many to imported food products. Although absence of accurate data makes it difficult to assess exact impact of the global financial and economic crises on poverty and employment, recent trends in growth rates confirm the adverse effect on the PICs. Per capita real income has fallen throughout the region. The adverse effects are manifested in lowering economic growth, reducing government revenues, increasing debt burdens, increasing cost of living, declining tourism, job losses and reduced remittances.

All Pacific countries, with the exception of Vanuatu, are net food importers. Furthermore, large segments of the population in the Pacific are net food buyers, not only in urban centres, but also in many rural areas. Atoll countries are exceedingly vulnerable to food insecurity and the impacts of volatile international food and energy prices due to inherent resource limitations, particularly productive land resources and water, in addition to geographic remoteness and isolation that increase the cost of shipping and communications. Higher expenditures on food and fuel have had consequential reductions in expenditure on health and education.

Economic growth rates in Pacific island countries have been generally modest (2.3 percent in 2009; forecast 3.7 percent in 2010).[7] The substantial

---

7   Asian Development Bank, 'Asian Development Outlook, 2010', Manila, 2010.

public sector outlays in development sectors in the last two decades and a generally positive growth trend (albeit modest) did not translate itself in any perceptible improvement in poverty or inequality. Recognizing that previous strategies have not yielded the expected growth, there is a broad consensus in the region that the PICs require a shift from dominantly 'public-sector-led' growth strategies of the past to public policies which will stimulate and diversify the productive sectors. This will, overtime, ensure: (i) increased resilience to external shocks; (ii) reduced pressure on land arising from rapid population growth; (iii) meeting the rising expectations of the people; and (iv) gradual reduction of dependence on continued external assistance.

Key growth sectors in the PICs are expected to be commercial fisheries, agricultural crops, tourism, small-scale manufacturing, and, for some of the larger countries, mineral/natural resources extraction. The natural resources endowment varies widely among the countries. The larger islands, the Solomon Islands and Fiji, are relatively rich in mineral resources, forests and oceanic fisheries. In contrast, the Polynesian and Micronesian islands are generally small and are less endowed with natural resources.

The region's major productive activities and their returns continued to be well below their potential. In fisheries, for example, of the US$2 billion in tuna extracted from the Pacific each year, just 3 percent accrues to Pacific countries in royalties and license fees.[8] Local ownership of vessels is limited, with foreign ships accounting for over 90 percent of the catch. With little local processing taking place, the PICs do not share in the additional US$2 billion-4 billion in value added to the tuna during processing and distribution.[9]

Table 3. Key Economic Indicators

Country	Current GDP (US$ million)	GDP per capita (US$)	Real GDP growth rate (%)			Inflation rate (%)		
	2009	2008	2008	2009	2010	2008	2009	2010
Cook Islands	183	10,907	1.2	-0.1	0.8	7.8	6.5	2.2
Fiji	3,500	4,264	0.2	-2.5	1.2	7.8	5.0	7.0
Kiribati	114	804	3.4	1.5	1.1	11.0	9.1	2.8
Marshall Islands	161	2,737	2.0	0.5	0.8	14.8	9.6	1.7
FS Micronesia	238	2,154	2.9	0.5	0.5	6.8	2.9	2.2
Nauru	22	2,396	1.0	1.0	0.0	4.5	1.8	1.8
Palau	164	8,812	1.0	-3.0	-1.0	12.0	5.2	3.0
Samoa	523	2,988	4.8	-5.5	-1.0	10.9	5.7	3.2
Solomon Islands	668	1,284	6.9	0.4	2.4	17.2	8.0	7.0
Tokelau	n.a.	n.a.	n.a.	n.a.	n.a.	n.a.	n.a.	n.a.
Tonga	259	2,891	1.2	2.6	1.9	14.5	12.3	6.1
Tuvalu	15	3,213	1.5	1.0	1.0	5.3	3.8	2.3
Vanuatu	554	2,388	6.6	3.0	3.5	4.8	4.3	3.0

Source: Asian Development Outlook, 2010.

---

8 World Bank, 'Evaluation of World Bank Assistance to Pacific Members Countries, 1992-2002', Operations Evaluation Department, Washington DC, March 2005, p.3.

9 Ibid.

In tourism, individual countries in the PICs receive fewer tourists compared to those received in similar island countries elsewhere in the world. Agricultural exports continue to comprise a narrow range of raw commodities, with only limited agro-processing taking place in most PICs. Remittances play an increasingly important role in the economies of the Pacific contributing towards economic growth and sustaining livelihoods, including meeting education and basic needs. Natural resources provide the mainstay for most Pacific island countries. Subsistence agriculture and fisheries are important determinants of food security, particularly in atolls where soils are generally poor and crop diversity is limited.

2.3 EQUITABLE ECONOMIC GROWTH AND POVERTY REDUCTION

Poverty as a concept was less of a priority policy concern in the Pacific a decade ago. But it has increasingly emerged as a significant issue in current years. Although it always existed in different forms underneath the social and family safety net, in recent years there has been progress in terms of measuring levels of poverty, i.e., a monetary value of poverty using the basic needs poverty line approach. This has made it possible to elevate the discussion with concrete facts and trends to the level of national policy dialogue culminating in public efforts to reduce levels of poverty.

Recent poverty-related data, when considered in conjunction with the results of participatory poverty assessments, points to a significant and growing problem in the region. The widely held perception that subsistence lifestyles, social networks and traditions provide a safety net against poverty in the PICs is increasingly being questioned. It is estimated that at least one third of the region's population lives in poverty and do not have sufficient income to satisfy their basic human needs. Some country-specific information is given below.

Notwithstanding data limitations, in Cooks Islands the number of people under the basic-needs national poverty line has remained the same during the period from 2006 to 2008, while in Fiji and FSM the number has increased during the period from 1990 to 2002 and remained the same to 2008. In FSM, the number of people under the national basic-needs national poverty line has increased during the period from 1998 to 2005. Other Pacific countries, with the exception of Vanuatu, have witnessed deterioration or no progress towards the achievement of the first target in MDG 1. Rapid urbanization and the growth of informal or under-serviced settlements lead to the urbanization of poverty in the Pacific. Tuvalu and Vanuatu have managed to reduce the number of people below national basic-needs poverty line significantly over the periods from 1994 to 2004 and 1998 to 2006, respectively.

Most national statistics and regional economic analyses[10] assert that Pacific countries initially have low levels of food poverty. This needs to be reconsidered as it is generally based on statistics collected before the recent food crisis in nearly all countries in the Pacific region. Despite the initial low levels of food deprivation in the region, most Pacific countries are still slightly off-track in terms of progress towards the achievement of the second target in MDG 1, which is eradicating extreme poverty and hunger. Governments in the Pacific region have scaled up efforts to improve the provision of basic services, such as health and education. Recent national MDG reports as well as regional reports still document a wide gap between income and human poverty in the Pacific region, pointing out the need for further improvement in the quality and coverage of services, particularly in rural and remote areas.

Employment: High and persistent unemployment, particularly among the youth, is a common phenomenon in the PICs. The 'poverty of opportunity' is considered the most prevalent form of

---

10 By bilateral donors (AusAID, NZAID), multilateral institutions (ADB, WB, UN system) and regional organizations (SPC, FIFs). Please see Annex 5 on documents consulted.

poverty in the region, particularly in the rural sector. This is manifested in increasing urban population and growing squatter settlements around major centres, leading to rising urban poverty. It is estimated that less than 25 percent of new graduates in the Pacific region find employment in the formal sector. In interpreting the employment figures and trends, one has to take into account the sizable informal sector and the prevalence of various types of traditional, non-conventional and non-monetary-wage employment.

2.4 MDGs AND HUMAN DEVELOPMENT

MDGs: According to the Pacific MDG report 2010, PICs have made significant effort towards achieving the MDGs, but some countries still have a long way to go. With another five years to reach the targets, the possibility seems real that some Pacific island nations will fall short in achieving the goals. The overall trend suggest that the Polynesian countries have been progressing relatively well, the Micronesian countries working hard to maintain gains in some areas and some of the Melanesian countries with a track record of conflict or civil/political tension are experiencing a loss of development gains made earlier. Stated below are some succinct findings from the MDG report.[11]

- Twelve Pacific Island States are off-track in reducing the portion of population under basic-needs national poverty line. Lack of up-to-date data and weak statistical capacity prevents accurate assessment of poverty (MDG 1) targets in the Pacific region. Economic growth is a necessary part of the solution to the problem, as are appropriate policies that target the needs of the poor.

- Primary school enrolment (MDG 2) is relatively high in the Pacific, although significant room for improvement remains in some countries. Ensuring that education effectively addresses both individual and societal needs remains a problem across the region.

- Women remain disadvantaged in many areas, including education, employment, and political representation. Overall, significant progress has been made towards equality and empowerment (MDG 3). Realization of gender goals requires identification of specific needs and implementation of policies and programmes to address them.

- Child and infant mortality (MDG 4) are declining in most of the region, but significant regional and subnational disparities remain. A continuing emphasis is needed on basic health care, including provision of immunizations, as well as more effective education regarding nutrition.

- Significant improvements have been made in maternal health (MDG 5) in recent decades, but this progress is not uniform across the region. Improving access to quality obstetric care – including emergency services – is the primary requirement for realizing further reductions in maternal mortality.

- The region's 'double burden of disease' (stemming from significant rates of both communicable and non-communicable diseases) has the potential to negatively affect social and economic development (MDG 6).

- The importance of environmental sustainability (MDG 7) is broadly recognized and widely reflected in both regional and national policies, but progress in implementing these policies is uneven. Accurate assessment of the state of the environment in the region is significantly hampered by problems with data quality and comparability. Some environmental issues facing the region are global in scope (e.g., global warming and associated sea level rise), and can only be effectively addressed through action by the international community.

Although the PICs continue to receive very high amounts of aid (in per capita terms), their share of global official development assistance (ODA)

---

11 Pacific Islands Forum Secretariat, '2010 Pacific Regional MDGs Tracking Report', Suva, July 2010.

Table 4. Human Development Index and Human Poverty Index Values (1998 and 2008)

Country	A. Human Development Index				B. Human Poverty Index			
	1998		2008		1998		2008	
	Index	Rank	Index	Rank	Index	Rank	Index	Rank
Cook Islands	0.822	2	0.829	1	6.1	3	3.7	1
Fiji	0.667	4	0.726	6	8.5	6	9.0	5
FS Micronesia	0.569	9	0.723	7	26.7	12	11.1	7
Kiribati	0.515	11	0.606	12	12.6	10	22.9	11
Marshall Islands	0.563	10	0.716	8	19.5	11	12.4	8
Nauru	0.663	5	0.652	10	12.1	9	15.0	9
Nieu	0.744	3	0.803	3	4.8	1	n.a.	n.a.
Palau	0.861	1	0.818	2	10.8	8	8.2	4
Samoa	0.590	7	0.770	4	8.6	7	5.1	3
Solomon Islands	0.371	13	0.566	13	49.1	14	31.3	12
Tokelau	n.a.	n.a.	n.a.	n.a.	7.6	5	n.a.	n.a.
Tonga	0.647	6	0.745	5	5.9	2	4.5	2
Tuvalu	0.583	8	0.700	9	7.3	4	9.2	6
Vanuatu	0.425	12	0.648	11	46.6	13	19.8	10

Note: HDI is a composite index of longevity, literacy and income. HPI represents poverty measured in all dimensions of HDI.
Source: United Nations, 'Pacific Sub-Region United Nations Development Assistance Framework (UNDAF) (2008-2012)', Mid Term Review, May-July 2010.

is declining, and major regional donors are directing a declining proportion of their assistance to PICs (MDG 8). The small size of their economies, remote locations, and lack of development and infrastructure make it difficult for PICs to be competitive in the global marketplace, and this is reflected by their collective US$2 billion trade deficit.

Human Development: The region demonstrated a steady improvement in human development. Between 1998 and 2008, Human Development Index (HDI) values in all countries, with the exception of Nauru and Palau, improved. There has been an insignificant change in ranking of the countries apart from Nauru, which has fallen by five places to tenth place. Among the others, Samoa's position has risen by three places to fourth, while Fiji moved down slightly to sixth place. In terms of the Human Poverty Index (HPI) values over the same period, nine of the 13 countries for which data is available show improvements in their levels of human poverty while four have worsened.

HDI and HPI indices together point to the fact that the human development and human poverty conditions in the Pacific region have been reasonably stable, except perhaps in Nauru. On the flip side there have not been any noticeable improvements either. The PICs will face challenges in the coming years with limited economic growth prospects and the severe resource and budgetary crunch. This will require the governments to give priority attention to policies that address human development conditions.

2.5 GOVERNANCE

Good governance has always been a sensitive issue in the Pacific, given the relative newness of the achievement of the independence by PICs and the importance attached to the traditional culture and value systems. However, in searching for reasons for inadequate economic growth and the perceived failure of the past development policies in the PICs, poor governance institutions and practices often appear as a key constraint. In many Pacific island countries the governance institutions critical for producing equitable and effective development are at different stages of maturity or development.

In the political context, there exists a mix of systems of governance. There are seven republics (with political parties, a Parliament, and the executive and judiciary): FS Micronesia, Kiribati, Marshall Islands, Nauru, Palau, Samoa, and Vanuatu; three constitutional monarchies, Solomon Islands, Tonga, and Tuvalu; one military regime (Fiji) and three autonomous and semi-autonomous systems of New Zealand's territories, Cook Islands, Niue, and Tokelau. There are also differences in the systems of internal governance; while most of the countries have a unitary and somewhat centralized system, where the government delegates powers to regional authorities, island councils or councils of elders, FS Micronesia is a federal government, sharing the power with the regional governments that have certain autonomous powers.

One distinctive feature in the Pacific islands is the coexistence of modern governance systems with the traditional governance structures. With differing views and values, this is an uneasy coexistence with degrees of inconsistencies and incoherence. The modern system is driven by values of individual merit, neutrality, equal participation, and the rights of the individual and the nuclear family. The traditional system, on the other hand, is built on values of loyalty and favour for kin and community, consensual and consultative values within the traditional hierarchy, and traditionally defined roles for men and women. The leaders in PICs are confronted with a difficult challenge of pursuing the public good and merit-based approaches in small societies with the countervailing strong and important traditional family and clan obligations. In response, there is a tendency for people in power in the Pacific islands to accord priority in distributing resources to constituents over generating long-term national growth. As a consequence, these factors can combine to contribute to create governance systems that tolerate corruption and encourage political instability, which in turn can undermine all efforts at development progress and economic growth.

An overview of the main elements of governance in the PICs is presented below for a better understanding of the context within which all socio-economic development initiatives are conducted. The observations are largely drawn from an Asian Development Bank cross-country study on governance in the Pacific[12] and UNDP information base on governance projects.

Legislature: Most of the legislatures in the PICs are young and still gaining their roles in governing the country. Meaningful or effective oversight of the executive branch by the legislature is generally lacking. This may be due to either lack of understanding of the role and process or limited formal education on the part of the parliamentarians.[13] Pacific legislatures currently suffer from various constraints: weak functioning secretariats to support legislators in their legislative and committee work; limited access to critical information and expertise needed for law-making and oversight; and inadequate systems and equipment. Consequently, legislators are often marginalized in the policy development, oversight and implementation process and have not been effectively engaged as development

---

12 Asian Development Bank, 'Governance in the Pacific: Focus for Action 2005-09', Manila, 2004.
13 Asian Development Bank, 'RETA 6065, Assessing Community Perspectives on Governance in the Pacific', Manila, 2002.

partners. In combination with an already weak institutional capacity, consistent and effective parliamentary oversight function is becoming increasingly difficult.

Executive branch and public administration: Policy development and decision-making in the executive branch of the government suffer from serious capacity weaknesses and system inadequacies. Policy analysis and evidence-based decision-making is generally not a requirement. Systems do not exist to enforce compliance with strategic direction or agreed national strategy. For example very few PICs require legal, environmental, and financial impact analysis of new policy and/or legislative proposals.

While weaknesses in policy formulation are evident in many of the PICs, inadequate policy implementation capacity and skills are of even more concern, as these often lead to inconsistent applications of approved policies. Neither category of inadequacy helps to create a predictable policy environment for citizens or external investors. Corruption in the public sector continues to be a major challenge in the region.

Oversight institutions: Institutions that oversee compliance and accountability in public service agencies, such as the offices of ombudsman and auditor-general, often suffer from inadequate resources and poorly trained staff which renders them ineffective. Non-compliance with government rules and regulations seems to be frequent. No strict regime of sanctions exists for disregarding rules and regulations including cases of gross financial irregularity and abuse of systems and authority.

The legal and regulatory framework: The existence of a fair legal and judicial system in a country is essential for protecting human rights and for resolving conflicts between citizens (including legal entities), and between citizens and the government. In most PICs, the legal and regulatory systems are generally weak and under-developed, due to the lack of skills and resources to enforce compliance, as well as the lack of predictability and transparency of policy decisions.

The judicial system: In most PICs, the judicial systems have a relatively better image and are viewed as generally independent, relatively less susceptible to corruption, and 'reasonably resourced'. Substantial shortfall exists in adequately trained and experienced judicial service personnel. Judicial systems are often hard hit by budgetary cutbacks, which have a stronger negative impact on access to justice by the poor and disadvantaged.

Decentralization: In most PICs, local governments have little capacity and limited funding relative to transferred responsibilities. There has been little devolution of power and authority. They receive meagre amount of funds from central governments, and generally lack the competence and the staff to design and implement programmes. The inability of the local governments to deliver services creates a negative image and crisis of confidence in the strength of participatory democracy among people at the grass root level.

Civil society, including community groups, provides a valuable link between governments and citizens and could be better used to enhance accountability of governments and public officials. In most PICs, effective mechanisms to encourage citizens' participation in the legislative process are generally lacking because information on the legislative agenda or draft bills are is rarely available in advance. Governance institutions and frameworks have not effectively prioritized the concerns of citizens, including disadvantaged groups.

2.6 ENVIRONMENT, CLIMATE CHANGE AND DISASTER

Pacific islanders have a close connection with the land, depending culturally, economically and spiritually on environmental resources, which provide both a built-in security and resource net for the subsistence population. A large numbers of islanders still depend directly on their environment. Traditional methods of governance have been supplemented with modern systems of management in many areas of civic and social life.

Introduction of lifestyle changes in urban areas has also introduced a variety of new environmental issues. As a consequence, environmental management has suffered. The dynamics of social and developmental changes has put tremendous pressure on fragile resources, negatively impacted the ability of populations to maintain a subsistence way of life, and caused environmental problems that hurt national development goals in tourism and local fisheries development. Irrespective of the diversity, the PICs share the following common environmental issues:

Land: Land is an extremely limited and vulnerable resource base in the PICs. It faces potential threats of degradation (more acutely in coastal areas), loss of productivity and intensive pressure. Loss of soil from development work and sediment buildup in lagoons as a result of construction or dredging has emerged as an issue.

Forests are diminishing at an unsustainable pace due to combination of population pressure, shifting cultivation, loss of traditional control.

Freshwater: Dwindling supply and quality of freshwater is a major issue in the PICs. The protection and conservation of supply and quality of water has become an increasingly important issue in the Pacific as the symptoms of global climate change are affecting rainfall variability in the region. Coral atolls depend entirely on rainwater, and recent lack of rain has recently caused Tuvalu to import drinking water. Population growth, urbanization and damage to water catchments as a result of rampant deforestation, inappropriate agricultural activities and inadequate waste disposal are all likely to have an increasing impact on water supplies throughout the region.

Sewage and waste disposal: With half to two-thirds of the population in many island nations now living in urban areas, problems of access to clean water and proper disposal of sewage and solid waste have also become critical problems in need of solutions. Outbreaks of disease – including cholera – as a result of poor waste management in some islands underlines the peril of poor or non-existent waste management practices. Pollution associated with rapid urbanization and crowded living conditions in cities and towns is emerging as a common phenomenon in many of the PICs.

Climate change poses a set of fundamental challenges to livelihoods and food security in the Pacific Islands region. The PICs recognize that the global warming caused by high carbon emissions from unsustainable production and consumption patterns in industrialized countries put them at increasing risk. Climate change and associated rising sea levels are of urgent concern for many Pacific countries. In the atoll nations of Tuvalu, Kiribati and the Marshall Islands climate change adaptation options are severely limited by the land area available. There is a risk, due to sea-level rise, that large numbers of people will be displaced from their present homes and livelihoods and forced to relocate to less vulnerable locations.

Coastal and marine resources: Pacific islanders are very dependent on coastal and marine resources, and the relatively large coastal zones of these small islands are highly vulnerable to environmental degradation. In addition, the development of marine resources, including commercial fishing and pearls, represents almost the sole opportunity for substantial economic development, especially for the atoll states. Imminent threats to the marine environment include nutrients derived from sewage, soil erosion and agricultural fertilizers; solid waste disposal; sedimentation; physical alterations caused by destruction of fringing reefs, beaches, wetlands and mangroves for coastal development.

Biodiversity of the region is very rich and comprises both land and marine biodiversity. Some islands have over 80 percent endemic species which occur nowhere else. Yet the biological diversity of Pacific islands is among the most critically threatened in the world, with up to 50 percent at risk. In fact, the Pacific has some of the highest extinction rates in the world. Biodiversity in the region is under pressure by large-scale logging, commercial agriculture, associated land clearing, and fires. The threats to marine biodiversity are alluded to in the preceding paragraph.

Environmental governance and institutional capacity: Weak environmental governance results in an inability of government monitoring agencies to mitigate potential development impacts on fragile environments. Across the PICs, the institutions for environmental planning and management are relatively new and have many capacity constraints. Hence, institutional capacity building remains a major priority for most governments.

The PICs participate in a range of Multilateral Environmental Agreement (MEA) processes which are key to building up resources and capacities to address the full range of environmental issues in the medium and long term. But these processes place substantial demands and significant additional stress on the capacities of a broad range of government agencies in the short run. The challenges include prioritizing environmental issues, coming to terms with a multitude of obligations imposed by the MEAs, and acquiring necessary financial and technical expertise. While there has been considerable development of global financing mechanisms, funds that have been channeled through global funding architecture have not been designed to accommodate the capacity constraints of small island states.

In general, the scale and scope of environmental challenges are increasing throughout the region. A big challenge to the government agencies is to integrate environmental concerns into their planning processes. An emerging and pressing need in the countries in the region is to develop and expand systems for incorporating environmental issues into the development planning process which will ensure sustainability of the future development and economic growth. The sustainability of fragile environments in the Pacific is under challenge because of the escalating problems of climate variability and climate change. The objective in the environmental sector strategy for the PICs is to develop the systems and processes in a way that ensures that environment management dimension is an integral part, not an afterthought, in any sector, programme or project planning process.

Disasters: The Pacific is one of the most disaster-prone regions in the world. Natural disasters have affected more than 3.4 million people and caused 1,747 fatalities (excluding Papua New Guinea) in the Pacific islands region since 1950. In some countries, more than 40 percent of the population is affected during a typical disaster year, e.g., Tonga and Samoa. The most prevalent disasters are cyclones, which accounted for 76 percent of reported disasters between 1950 and 2004, followed by earthquakes, droughts and floods. In 2010 alone, Fiji and the Pacific islands faced emergencies that included five tropical cyclones, two volcanic eruptions and one tsunami. High exposure to climate risks and limited adaptive capacity make Pacific island countries particularly vulnerable to climate change and sea-level rise. It is therefore necessary to view climate change and disaster risk reduction issues in an integrated manner.

The national institutional mechanisms and structures for early warning and disaster response in the PICs are relatively new phenomena. The increased awareness and responsibility of the governments in this respect is taking shape through creation of new organized systems and processes. The increasing role of communities and civil society to work alongside the government in pre- and post-disaster period is being recognized and brought into a new regime of disaster response in some countries.

2.7 PEACE AND STABILITY

The Pacific is characterized by a vast diversity of religious, traditional, and formal governance structures and is undergoing rapid social, economic and political changes. While there is a long tradition of peace and stability in the region, in recent times, the incidence and pervasiveness of social tensions, conflict and violence has increased. These phenomena manifest themselves in a wide variety of forms – including high levels of inter-tribal/racial violence, increasing crimes and urban violence, social ethno-religious tensions, and corruption. While the causes of violence and the triggering factors differ from country to country and, at times, at sub-national levels, common elements include existence of cultural differences among different population groups, weak governance capacities and institutions unable to mediate change and tensions in non-violent ways. The underlying cause sometimes is also related to the process and outcome of development as well. The Biketawa Declaration agreed upon by the Pacific leaders sets out eight good governance principles and outlines an approach to regional intervention in times of conflict. The Regional Assistance Mission to the Solomon Islands (RAMSI) is based on this Declaration.

2.8 GENDER EQUALITY

Gender inequality undermines long-term development in the Pacific. Culturally, there are variations on the role and place of women among the three subregions, Melanesia, Polynesia and Micronesia, which account for differences in the situation of women and girls. Traditionally, all Pacific societies were characterized by social rank, while in Melanesia, societies were ranked by gender (Solomon Islands, Vanuatu and parts of Fiji) resulting in greater gender inequality. In Polynesia and Micronesia, women of rank are not equal to their male peers, but outrank males of lesser status.[14] In spite of some cultural differences, all countries are characterized by a lesser role for women and the dominance of men in control of economic and political assets – even where there are no legal barriers to women's land ownership or political representation.[15]

While gender equality in school enrolments is generally positive, concerns lie elsewhere: violence against women is very widespread, especially in Melanesia, women's participation in political leadership is among the lowest in the world, and multiple barriers to economic participation and empowerment of women remain (for example with regard to ownership of land).

The Pacific has the lowest rate of women's representation in national parliaments worldwide, with several PICs having no or only one female MP at the national level, and low levels of representation at local levels of government. The regional average for the proportion of women in national legislative bodies in the Pacific states (excluding Australia and New Zealand) stands at a mere 2.5 percent, a trend that has not changed in the past decade. Several countries – the Federated States of Micronesia, Nauru, the Solomon Islands – have no women in Parliament.

Recent studies using World Health Organization methodology have revealed very high rates of violence against women in the PICs, including crimes of sexual violence during times of political instability or natural disasters. In Kiribati,[16] for example, the study found that 68 percent of women aged 15-49 who had ever been in a relationship had experienced some form of violence (emotional, physical and/or sexual), from an intimate partner; 90 percent had experienced controlling behaviour from a male partner; and 10 percent had faced violence from a non-partner.[17] In Solomon Islands, a study based on

---

14 Meleisea, P.S. and Meleisea, E. 'The Elimination of All Forms of Discrimination and Violence against the Girl Child: Situation Paper for the Pacific Island Region', prepared for UNIFEM and UNICEF, 2003, pp. 6-7.

15 While women are eligible to run for office throughout the region, there are still obstacles: for example, in Samoa, only matais (chiefs) can be elected and only one in ten matais are women; in Tonga, 17 seats are open for general election, nine are reserved for nobles who are all male, and up to four can be appointed by the king.

16 These results were found in spite of the old matrilineal traditions.

17 Rasanathan, J.J.K. and Bhushan, A., 'Measuring and Responding to Gender-based Violence in the Pacific: Action on Gender Inequality as a Social Determinant of Health', Republic of Kiribati, WHO Regional Office for the Western Pacific, October 2011, p. 4.

the same methodology, found that 64 percent of women aged 15-49 who had ever had an intimate partner had experienced some kind of violence by the partner, and when violence was experienced, it was more likely to be severe than moderate or mild. Eighteen percent of women had experienced non-partner violence, and 37 percent had been sexually abused before the age of 15.[18] The cause of gender-based violence is attributed to inequality, although of course it also reinforces it. Gender-based violence takes a heavy toll on women's health and wellbeing, as well as on their productivity and participation in their communities.

The study added, in the case of the Solomon Islands that any achievements in addressing gender-based violence were erased by civil conflict from 1998 to 2003: "After the 2003 peace agreements, partner violence increased, survivors were stigmatized, perpetrators largely enjoyed impunity, and little action was taken on stated commitments to counter gender-based violence." Similar setbacks for women, including increased sexual violence and impunity, were found following conflict in Fiji.[19]

All countries have ratified the Convention on the Elimination of All Forms of Discrimination against Women (CEDAW) with the noticeable exception of Tonga, and Palau – although the latter has just signed the agreement (September 2011). A 2007 study by UNIFEM and the Pacific Centre analysed legislative compliance to the convention based on 113 indicators and found results ranging such as: Fiji, full compliance with 49, to non-compliance with 39: Samoa full compliance with 40, non-compliance with 49; FS Micronesia, full compliance with 26, non-compliance with 69.[20]

Security Council Resolution 1325 takes on greater significance given the actual (Solomon Islands, Fiji) periods of violence, as well as potential future violence in the region. Besides protection for women and girls in conflict, the Security Council Resolution 1325 requires meaningful participation of women in decision making around peacebuilding and governance in order to strengthen their say in issues that affect them. This is a particular challenge in a region where women are already vastly under-represented in decision-making. While women were active in peacemaking and reconciliation during the conflict in Solomon Islands, the government has been criticized for paying little attention to increasing women's involvement in the formal process of conflict management and in decision making in the post-conflict phase.[21]

2.9 DEVELOPMENT COOPERATION AND AID EFFECTIVENESS

Official development assistance (ODA) plays a critical role in helping the PICs in their efforts to achieve progress in the implementation of their development goals. Historically, the Pacific islands region is a major recipient of development assistance. The large flow of ODA measured in per capita terms is estimated at about seven times the average for all developing countries. However, this comparatively high flow corresponds with very high per capita costs of establishing service delivery and infrastructure in small island countries.

The flows of development assistance are of critical importance to the budgets and the implementation of development strategies of most PICs. In fact, for many island countries ODA is a lifeline

---

18 Ibid., p.3.

19 AusAID, 'Violence Against Women in Melanesia and East Timor: Building on Global and Regional Promising Approaches', Department of Development Effectiveness, Canberra, 2008, p. 153.

20 Jivan, V. and Forster, C. 'Translating CEDAW Into Law: CEDAW Legislative Compliance in Nine Pacific Island Countries', UNDP Pacific Centre and UNIFEM Pacific Regional Office, Suva, 2006, pp v-vi.

21 NGO Working Group on Women, Peace and Security, 'A Call to Ensure Women's Participation in Resolving the Conflict in the Solomon Islands', Press Release, New York, 12 May 2006.

for income and support. Across the board, there is a lack of comprehensive monitoring of the value of the financial flows and the resulting development outcomes.

Despite its high levels, there is still a concern with the role of development assistance in developing self-sustaining economies in the region. A number of reviews point out that consequences of high levels of ineffectively utilized or misdirected aid exacerbate the existence of large public sectors, overvalued exchange rates, high prices, high wages, corruption, poor infrastructure, and weak capacity in governments. At the same time, positive impacts of external aid can be discerned. Some donor reviews argue that the situation in the Pacific 'would be far worse' without ongoing assistance. External assistance has generally supported public sector outlay in development initiatives, which helped improving social indicators.

Through the focus on the Forum's Eight Principles of Good Governance, the Paris and Pacific Principles of Aid Effectiveness and the Cairns Compact, there has been a wide recognition that the solution for many development problems may be achieved through better political leadership and improved governance. Clear examples of good practices that have been implemented in some PICs and could be replicated elsewhere have been listed in the outcomes of the June 2010 Regional Aid Effectiveness Workshop. The Pacific Conference on the Human Face of the Global Economic Crisis held in Vanuatu in February 2010 recognized the importance of the principles of aid effectiveness for the PICs as agreed at the various High Level Forums on Aid Effectiveness (Paris 2005, and Accra 2008); the PICs/Development Partners Meeting in Palau (2007); and the 40th Pacific Islands Forum's Cairns Compact on Strengthening Development Coordination in the Pacific (2009).

Australia continues to be the single largest donor to the region providing 55 percent of all aid flow. In 2009 total external aid to the region amounted to US$ 1,166 million.[22] Other major donors include New Zealand, the US (the Compact Funding Agreement is the largest source of income for the Micronesian countries of Marshall Islands, Federated States of Micronesia, and Palau) and the EU which each contribute between 10-15 percent of total aid to the region. Japan and increasingly the People's Republic of China (PRC) are major donors that mostly concentrate on the provision of equipment, and turnkey infrastructure and constructions projects. Taiwan (not included in ODA listing) provides substantial assistance to Nauru, Kiribati and Tuvalu. The UN system assistance in 2009 amounted to approximately US$28.8 million, which accounted for around 2.5 percent of total aid to the region.

Trade: The PICs are in the process of establishing mechanisms to implement the Pacific Island Countries Trade Agreement (PICTA), which aims to create a common market and increase trade within the region. The Melanesian Spearhead Group Trade Agreement and the EU/ACP Cotonou Agreement, including the Economic Partnership Agreements (EPA), are also designed to promote further duty-free trade between the parties. Capacity building for trade policy is being supported under the EPA and also through UNDP's Integrated Framework for Trade initiative focused on the Least Developed Countries (LDCs). In addition, PICs are considering the impending trade negotiations under the Pacific Agreement on Closer Economic Relations (PACER) Plus with Australia and New Zealand. Pacific development partners need to deliver on commitments to substantially increase technical, financial and political support for aid for trade and the Enhanced Integrated Framework initiative. Aid for trade could be especially helpful to the PICs in providing finance for export-oriented

---

22 From United Nations, 'Sustainable Development in the Pacific: Progress and Challenges', Pacific Regional Report for the 5 Year Review of the Mauritius Strategy for Further Implementation of the Barbados Programme of Action for Sustainable Development of SIDS (MSI+5), ESCAP Subregional Office for the Pacific, Suva, April 2010.

Table 5. Official Development Assistance for Pacific Island Countries and Aid Flows by Donors (2009)

A. Official Development Assistance

Country	ODA (US$ Millions)	ODA per capita (US$)	% of GDP
Cook Islands	9.3	461	4
Fiji	57.5	69	2
Kiribati	27.1	285	35
Marshall Islands	52.1	894	35
FS Micronesia	114.9	1,035	49
Nauru	125.6	2,912	13
Niue	14.8	5,514	88
Palau	22.3	1,108	14
Samoa	37.5	207	7
Solomon Islands	246.1	497	63
Tokelau	n.a.	n.a.	n.a.
Tonga	30.9	302	12
Tuvalu	11.7	1,197	44
Vanuatu	56.7	251	13
Regional Aid	138.7	n.a.	n.a.
Total	1,165.9	136	9

B. Aid Flows by Donors

Development Partner	Aid (US$ Millions)
Australia	649.3
Canada	8.2
European Union	143
France	16.7
Global Fund	10.8
International Financial Institutions	9.9
Japan	70.3
New Zealand	120.9
United Kingdom	5.4
United Nations and Multilateral Institutions	28.8
United States	171.7
Other	2.5

Source: United Nations, 'Sustainable Development in the Pacific: Progress and Challenges', Pacific Regional Report for the 5 Year Review of the Mauritius Strategy for Further Implementation of the Barbados Programme of Action for Sustainable Development of SIDS (MSI+5), ESCAP Subregional Office for the Pacific, Suva, April 2010.

infrastructure (e.g., roads, ports and power) to support a strengthening in their export competitiveness.

Debt: It is recognized that the debt position of many PICs has worsened as a result of the global economic crisis. In many cases, this is a result of governments maintaining critical expenditure in the face of declining tax revenues. It was noted in the outcome statement of the Pacific Conference on the Human Face of the Global Economic Crisis: "Debt relief will enable some Pacific countries to focus more resources on social vulnerabilities. At the regional level, options to help high debt Pacific countries cope with and ultimately overcome structural weaknesses could be considered."

However, no PIC has yet been classified as a Highly Indebted Poor Country (HIPC) in terms of MDG8 and thus no debt relief initiatives have been activated. According to the latest IMF Article IV Reports, the highest levels of external debt among the PICs are with Marshall Islands and Tonga where external debt is projected to reach 54.6 percent and 50.7 percent of GDP in 2010 respectively.

Chapter 3
THE UNITED NATIONS AND UNDP IN THE PACIFIC

3.1 UNDP OVERVIEW AND STRUCTURE

UNDP is highly visible in the Pacific and since 2003, it has adapted its strategy and approach in responding to a myriad of challenges facing the region. There are currently 17 UN agencies,[23] programmes and offices working in the Pacific subregion. In Fiji, there are 13 UN agencies, programmes and offices and in Samoa there are six. Each UN body has its own representative, head or coordinator.

The UN Offices work together with UN Country Teams (UNCTs) to coordinate the work of UN fund agencies and organizations in support of the achievement of national development goals, which are reflected in the Millennium Declaration and MDGs as well as to assist governments to respond to emergencies and national security issues.

UNDP Multi-Country Offices: UNDP has three country offices in the Pacific located in Fiji, Samoa and Papua New Guinea, led by UN Resident Coordinators who are representatives of the UN Secretary-General in the country. Both Fiji and Samoa operate separate Multi-Country Offices which cover 14 Pacific Island Countries[24] while PNG has its own country office in Port Moresby. A sub-office of the UNDP Fiji MCO was established in the Solomon Islands capital, Honiara, in September 2007 because the development crisis required a more direct presence of UNDP.[25]

UNDP Pacific Centre: The Pacific Centre, based in Suva, serves the two Multi-Country Offices based in Fiji and Samoa, and the sub-office in Solomon Islands. As part of the regional structure of the Asia Pacific bureau it also has responsibility to provide technical support to the Papua New Guinea office. The Pacific Centre provides technical backstopping, monitoring and evaluation expertise in the delivery of country-based activities including training and workshops, project design, assessments, implementation and evaluation. It also delivers specific regionally focused activities to develop regional and national capacities and promote regional cooperation and coordination. It manages the UNDP subregional project portfolios for the Pacific. The Centre's resources are allocated in its annual work plan following a performance review process, which includes feedback from its Management Committee and a regional Advisory Committee. The Centre ensures that its work is targeted and reflects the comparative advantage of UNDP.

Significantly, the Regional Centre in Bangkok is also mandated to provide technical and policy advisory support to the Pacific as well as Asia and while most of this is deferred to the Pacific Centre, there are aspects of the Pacific Centre's work which is supported from Bangkok (energy and environment) and, until recently, HIV and AIDS. The Pacific is also expected to benefit from aid management, knowledge management and gender equality

---

23 FAO, ILO, ISDR, IFAD, OHCHR, UNAIDS, UNESCAP, UNDP (including the Pacific Centre), UNESCO, UNFPA, UNICEF, UNIFEM, UNHCR, UNOCHA, UNOPS, WHO and WMO. More UN agencies are expected to join the UNCTs in Fiji and Samoa, such as IFAD.

24 The Fiji MCO covers 10 Pacific Island Countries (Fiji, Kiribati, Marshall Islands, FS Micronesia, Nauru, Palau, Solomon Islands, Tonga, Tuvalu, and Vanuatu), while the Samoa MCO serves four PICs (Cook Islands, Niue, Samoa, Tokelau).

25 A Project Implementation Unit was initially established in 2002 and it evolved into a fully fledge sub-office in 2007. This is the only UNDP sub-office in the Pacific region and has a Deputy Resident Representative.

support from Bangkok where senior professional colleagues in these fields are located.

Joint Presences: In order to enhance their assistance to individual countries, UNDP, UNICEF and UNFPA offices initiated in 2006 the Pacific UN Joint Presences. The Joint Presences is an initiative of the three organizations to work together on programmes in eight selected countries.[26]

The Joint Presences came about as a result of the response to the demands of a number of PICs which requested to bringing the UN closer to home. The countries wanted to have a UN representative on the ground, to which they could ask questions and ensure that questions were answered in an efficient and timely manner. Likewise, the UN saw this initiative as a means of also creating a much closer link to the government in also ensuring that queries were met from governments in an efficient and timely fashion.

Through the Joint Presences, UNDP takes the lead in hosting UNICEF and UNFPA in Tuvalu, Solomon Islands, Nauru and Palau, UNICEF leads in hosting the other two agencies in Kiribati and Vanuatu and UNFPA leads in hosting the two agencies in RMI and FSM. Country Development Managers[27] (CDM) who are either qualified local professionals of the country or internationally recruited UNVs manage the day-to-day affairs of the Joint Presences Office. They are the liaison between the governments, CSOs and development partners in their countries and the UN. In Tonga UNDP is upgrading its field presence to another Joint Presences in consultation with UNICEF and UNFPA, bringing the total number of Joint Presences[28] to nine.

3.2 UN DEVELOPMENT ASSISTANCE FRAMEWORK (UNDAF)

In 2003, key agencies including UNDP, UNFPA and UNICEF developed separate UNDAF for five of the LDCs of the region (Samoa,[29] Kiribati, Solomon Islands, Tuvalu, and Vanuatu). However, it switched to a regional UNDAF for the 2008-2012 programme cycle to obtain greater programme cohesion and harmonization among UN agencies.[30]

The 2008-2012 UNDAF for the Pacific subregion sets out the strategic focus for the UN's dialogue with the PICs for the period. It is the product of partnerships between the UN Country Teams of Fiji and Samoa and the 15 UN agencies, programmes and offices in the Pacific, and is driven by the needs and priorities of governments of 14 PICs.

The four key priorities embodied in the Pacific UNDAF 2008-2012 framework was developed in consultation with governments, civil society and development partners and allows the UN to work with Pacific governments and its people under following priorities or 'outcomes':

1. **Equitable economic growth and poverty reduction,** by supporting the development and implementation of evidence-based, regional, pro-poor National Sustainable Development Strategies to address population, poverty and economic exclusion issues,

---

26 These include Solomon Islands, Kiribati, Vanuatu, Federated States of Micronesia (FSM), the Republic of Nauru, the Republic of the Marshall Islands (RMI), Palau and Tuvalu.

27 The CDMs include Sharon Sakuma (Palau), Aren Teannaki (Kiribati), Okean Ehmes (FSM), Terry Keju (RMI), Roselyne Arthur (Vanuatu) and Tatiana Prokhorova (Nauru). Recruitment of CDM for Tuvalu is in process by UNDP and UNDP is upgrading its field presence in Tonga.

28 It is noted that although Samoa parish did not initiate any Joint Presences, the MCO did make concerted efforts under a very limited resource based from the PRTTF, to explore the placement of National Strategic Planners in the Cook Islands and Niue to mainstream MDGs and gender into NISP/NSDP respectively.

29 Samoa is due to graduate from a non-LDC status in 2013.

30 In 1997, the United Nations Secretary-General launched a campaign to bring the UN system together to achieve common development goals. This was the beginning of UN reform with the goal of Delivering as One piloted in eight countries in 2007.

stimulate equitable growth, create economic opportunities and decent employment, and promote sustainable livelihoods.

2. **Good governance and human rights,** by enhancing national and regional governance systems that exercise the principles of inclusive good governance, respecting and upholding human rights; and supporting the development of resilient Pacific island communities participating in decision-making at all levels.

3. **Equitable social and protection services,**[31] through support to the development of evidence-based and inclusive policies and plans; improved systems to deliver accessible, affordable, well-managed, gender-sensitive quality social and protection services; and individual and community behaviour that reflects healthy lifestyles, social protection and better use of social services.

4. **Sustainable environmental management,** by mainstreaming of environmental sustainability and renewable energy into regional and national policies, planning frameworks and programmes; and supporting Pacific communities to sustainably use their environment, natural resources and cultural heritage.

The UN has estimated that it will be able to mobilize and contribute around US$309.7 million overall to UNDAF 2008-2012 outcomes, directing approximately US$93.8 million towards economic growth and poverty reduction, US$38.3 million towards good governance and human rights, US$95.3 million towards equitable social and protection services, and US$60.3 million towards sustainable environmental management. Its current focus is on the five LDCs in the region, directing roughly 58 percent of its resources to the LDCs and 42 percent to the nine non-LDCs.

3.3 UNDP MULTI-COUNTRY PROGRAMMES

UNDP supports the PICs through three programmes approved by the Executive Board of UNDP, namely:

- Multi-country programme, operated by the Multi-Country Office (MCO) located in Fiji, covering Federated States of Micronesia, Fiji, Kiribati, Nauru, Palau, the Republic of the Marshall Islands, Solomon Islands, Tonga, Tuvalu, and Vanuatu.

- Multi-country programme, operated by the MCO located in Samoa, covering Cook Islands, Niue, Samoa and Tokelau.

- Asia-Pacific regional programme which includes projects and activities supporting Pacific island countries individually or collectively, operated by the Asia-Pacific Regional Centre in large part through its Pacific Centre.

To operationalize these programmes, UNDP enters into an agreement to implement the Country Programme Action Plan (CPAP) with the Government of each country. Through these programmes, UNDP provides policy advice, capacity development, advocacy and other operational activities with a view to facilitating the attainment of MDGs, poverty reduction, and democratic governance, sustainable use of environment and energy, prevention of and recovery from conflicts and disaster, and other goals of UNDP such as gender equality. For the current programme cycle of 2008-2012, the two multi-country programmes operated by MCOs in Fiji and Samoa were developed in full alignment with UNDAF 2008-2012.

---

31 Equitable social and protection services include education, health, water and environmental sanitation, nutrition, population, injuries and protection (including rehabilitation and integration services).

3.3.1 FIJI MULTI-COUNTRY PROGRAMME DOCUMENT (MCPD)

2003-2007 MCPD

UNDP support was prioritized under three related areas:

- **Poverty reduction and sustainable livelihoods for MDG achievement:** facilitating financial services for the poor in Fiji, Vanuatu and Marshall Islands; policy development for inclusive growth and globalization in Palau, Marshall Islands and Federated States of Micronesia; sustainable livelihoods in Marshall Islands.

- **Democratic governance and human rights** through parliamentary strengthening in Fiji, Solomon Islands and Marshall Islands; decentralization and local governance in Tuvalu and Kiribati; participatory democracy and civic education in Tonga; peace and stability in Fiji and Solomon Islands; human rights advocacy for policy development and community education, and HIV/AIDS across the region.

- **Environmental protection and resource management** through programmes in environmental governance, climate change, biodiversity, energy and waste management with differentiated focus in the 10 PICs. A key focus has been on assisting countries to meet their obligations under various multilateral and regional environment agreements.

2008-2012 MCPD

Taking into account lessons learned in the past programming cycle, the MCPD 2008-2012 seeks to respond to current and emerging development challenges of the PICs, through continued emphasis on capacity development; stronger partnerships at the national level and robust engagement and coordination with key stakeholders; strategic programmatic focus and leveraging of regular resources in high impact areas; and strengthening regional and national linkages to support the Pacific Plan.

In alignment with the UNDAF, the goal of the MCPD is to achieve the MDGs through building resilient and inclusive societies, based on the following four key inter-related outcome areas across the 10 countries:

- **Outcome 1. Poverty reduction and the Millennium Development Goals.** UNDP would assist the PICs to stimulate inclusive economic growth and promote sustainable livelihoods through support to: (a) formulation and implementation of national and sectoral plans and strategies aligned with MDGs, (b) strengthening capacity of national statistical systems to generate disaggregated poverty data and analyses; (c) improving aid management systems linking to national plans and budgets; (d) facilitation of inclusive and equitable trade mechanisms, private-sector partnerships, employment-generation policies and enhancing financial competencies; and (e) multi-sectoral planning and leadership capacity development to enhance the engagement of communities and decision-makers at all levels to take immediate action on HIV and AIDS.

- **Outcome 2. Good governance and human rights.** UNDP would strengthen national policy capacities and governance systems through specific programmatic activities geared towards principles of good leadership and accountability; enhancing awareness of human rights and the availability of mechanisms to claim them. The focus would be on enhancing participatory democracy through civic and human rights education; decentralized governance for development and participatory decision-making; and parliamentary support, based on evolving priorities and demands of the Pacific countries.

- **Outcome 3. Crisis prevention and recovery.** UNDP would assist countries to strengthen capacity to prevent and manage crises and build resilience to the impact of tensions and disasters through support to the development of integrated approach to addressing and reducing vulnerability to tension and disaster, effective recovery strategies to address the root causes of humanitarian crises and natural disasters; and addressing the long-term livelihood needs of communities.

- **Outcome 4. Environment and sustainable management.** UNDP would support a more resilient region with strengthened capacity for sustainable management of environment and natural resources through: (a) the mainstreaming of environmental sustainability and sustainable energy into national policies, planning frameworks and programmes (in all countries of the Pacific); and (b) strengthening institutional support. The focus would be on environmental governance, including promotion of sustainable renewable energy and adaptation to climate change into national strategies, as well as improving access to and management of MEAs.

- Cross-cutting themes and joint programmes. UNDP programming will address the linkages between these four objectives, and mainstream key cross-cutting themes into country-specific priorities. This includes the promotion of human rights and protecting the dignity and integrity of all people; and gender equity, guided by the CEDAW.

3.3.2 SAMOA MULTI-COUNTRY PROGRAMME DOCUMENT

2003-2007 MCPD

Under the 2003-2007 Country Programme for Samoa and the Multi-Country Programme for the Cook Islands, Niue and Tokelau, UNDP supported the implementation of national development plans in all four countries. National and community-based programmes were developed and implemented in three related areas:

- MDG achievement and human poverty reduction,
- Democratic governance, and
- Environment and energy for sustainable development.

2008-2012 MCPD

The MCPD outcome areas are set out below:

- **Equitable economic growth and poverty reduction:** through a United Nations joint programme on national planning for MDG achievement, UNDP would focus its support on MDG 1 (eradicating poverty) and MDG 3 (empowering women).

- **Good governance and human rights:** through its global advocacy role, mandates, convening power and status in the international community.

- **Crisis prevention and recovery:** based on its global mandate to support gender-responsive disaster risk reduction, UNDP, in close collaboration with the United Nations Disaster Management Team and the UNDP Bureau of Crisis Prevention and Recovery, aimed to attain the following results: gender-responsive disaster risk management plans at community level; national disaster response systems strengthened and systems in place for capacity development, national drills and strengthened response in all countries.

- **Sustainable environmental management:** through its national, regional and global partnerships for sustainable development, UNDP would help to achieve MDG 7 (environmental sustainability).

To implement the MCPD 2008-2012 across the four programme areas, approximate resource requirement was projected at $27,306,000, of which UNDP regular resources allocated was $4,136,000. These indicative figures are likely to change as programmes evolve over time.

3.4 UNDP RESULTS AND RESOURCES FRAMEWORK

Since 2003, Fiji and Samoa MCOs have been able to build on and strengthen their results-oriented framework. An overview of the results areas have been highlighted above and an overview of resources allocated in different areas of focus

Figure 2. Samoa MCO Delivery

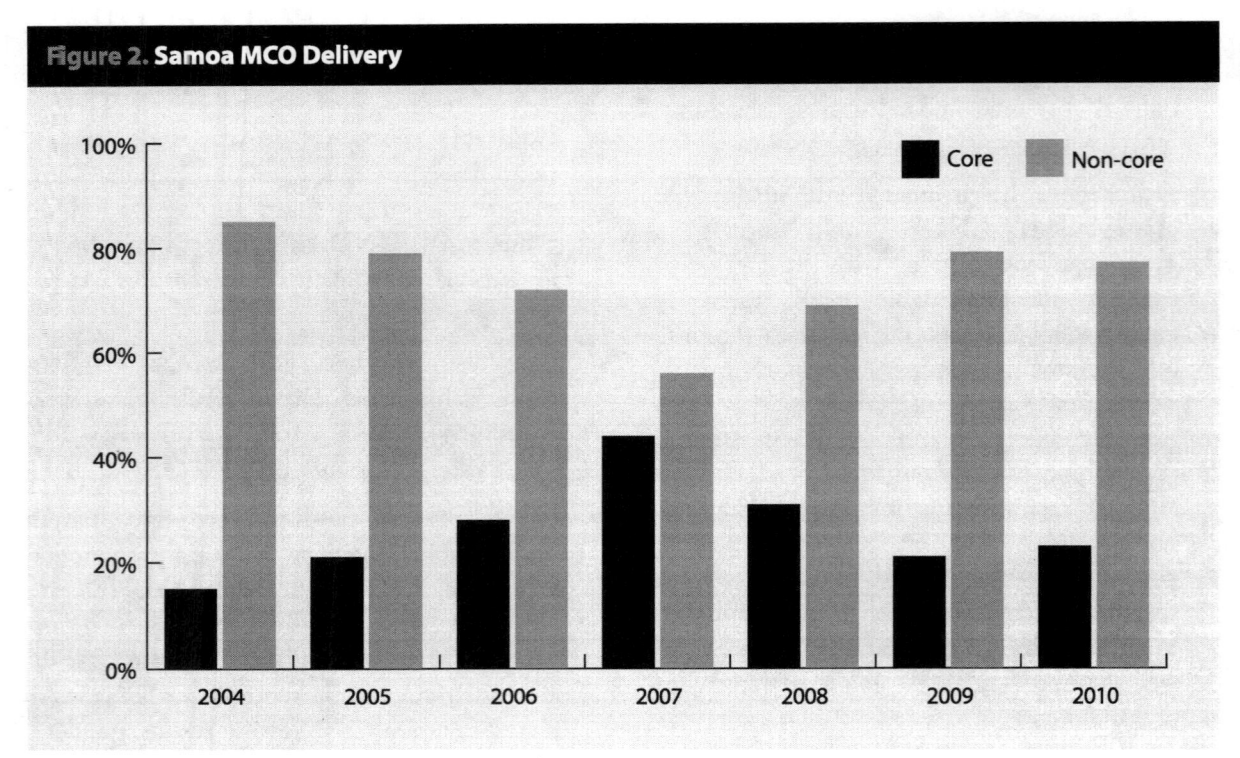

Source: Samoa MCO 2011, UNDP

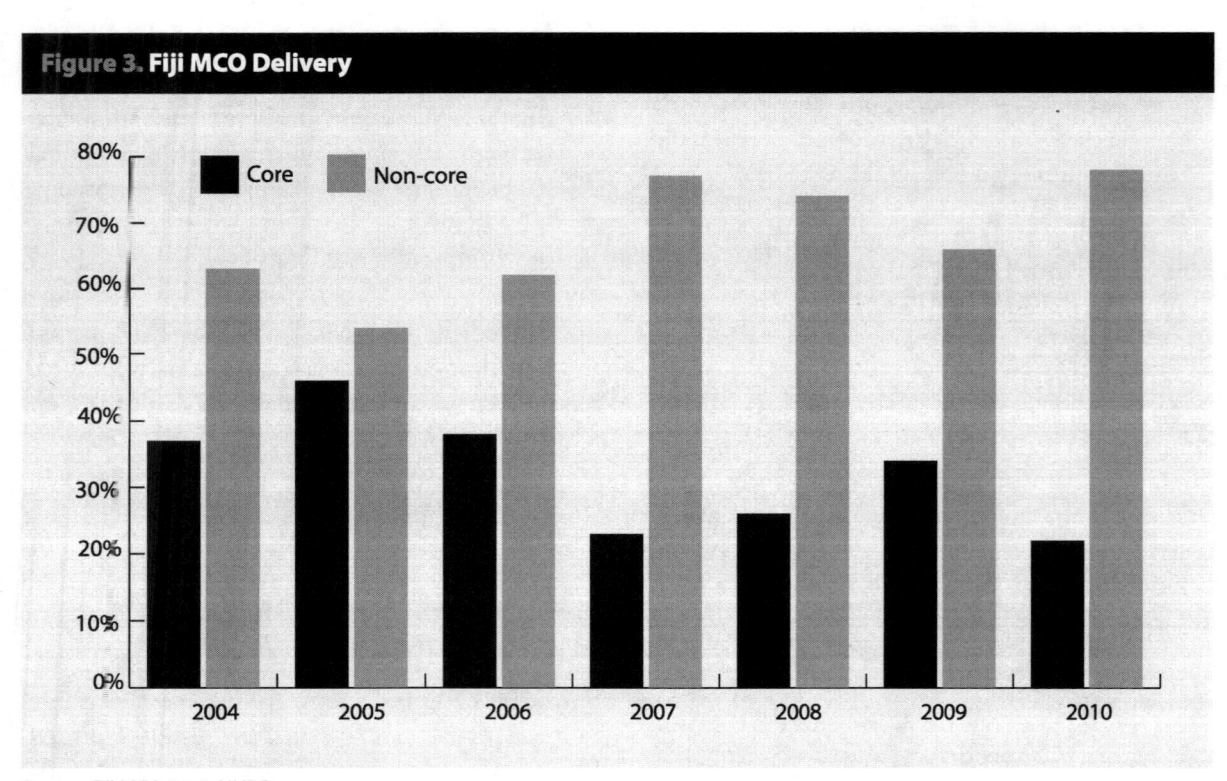

Figure 3. Fiji MCO Delivery

Source: Fiji MCO 2011, UNDP

Figure 4. Pacific Centre Delivery

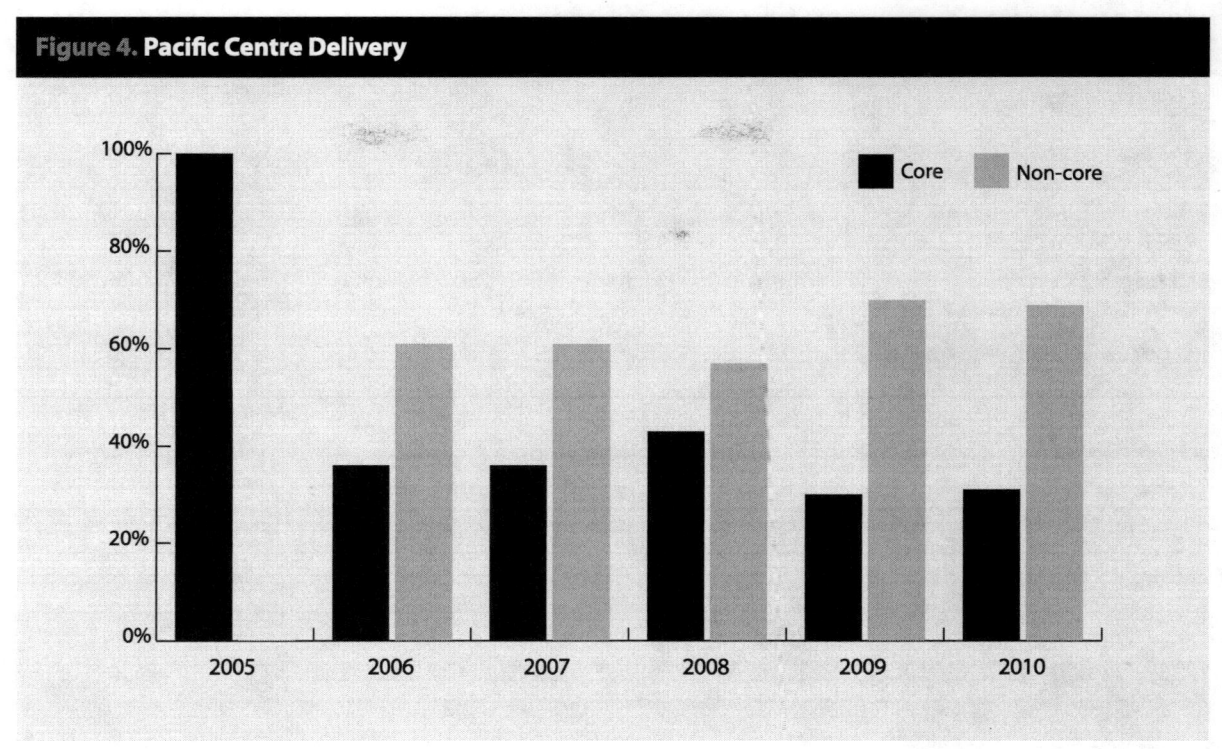

Source: Pacific Centre MCO 2011, UNDP

are given below. Collaborations with key development partners have been enhanced through its targeted development assessment framework. This has been evident with the flow of non-core resources being channeled via UNDP MCOs.

Figures 2-5 represent the critical importance of non-core (donor and cost sharing) resources for both the MCOs and the Pacific Centre. They demonstrate the effectiveness of the partnership that UNDP has been able to nurture with donor partners. It is reassuring to observe that UNDP still enjoys high confidence of donors and development partners, and has leveraged its comparative advantage to deliver substantial programmes in the PICs. It also reflects potential downside vulnerability in case there is a contraction of sources or changes in donor policies. For UNDP to be able to deliver a sizeable programme for impact, it will continue to be reliant on non-core resources.

For the 2004-2010 period, non-core resources contributed an average annual 74 percent of the total delivery for the Samoa MCO. For the same period, the average annual contribution of non-core resources to the Fiji MCO was 68 percent of the total delivery. The Pacific Centre average annual non-core resource was 54 percent during 2005-2010.

Based on the level of core and non-core funding that is secured by MCOs, the resources are then allocated to agreed country and regional priority needs in each of the respective Country Programme of Action. A consolidated analysis of the MCO budgets and expenditure between 2004 and 2010 indicates overall expenditures within each of the key outcomes areas were within the allocated budgets.

Key trends highlighted in the consolidated expenditure for the MCOs indicate the following:

- Fiji MCO top two priorities based on value of allocated budget and expenditures were in Outcome 4 – Crisis Prevention and Recovery (38 percent) and Outcome 3 – Environment Sustainable Management (31 percent).

Table 6. Consolidated Expenditure of Fiji and Samoa MCOs (2004-2010, US$ Millions)

Practice Area	Fiji MCO 2004-2010			Samoa MCO 2004-2010		
	Budget	Expenditure	Rate of Utilization	Budget	Expenditure	Rate of Utilization
Outcome 1: Achieving MDGs and Reducing Poverty	8,797	5,188	59%	3,431	1,331	39%
Outcome 2: Fostering Democratic Governance	17,051	11,362	67%	4,758	2,580	54%
Outcome 3: Environment and Sustainable Management	29,104	20,708	71%	3,642	2,353	65%
Outcome 4: Crisis Prevention and Recovery	36,899	24,862	67%	30,728	19,378	63%
Not entered	7,609	4,241	56%	894	567	63%
Total	**99,460**	**66,361**	**67%**	**43,453**	**26,209**	**60%**

Source: UNDP Fiji and Samoa MCO

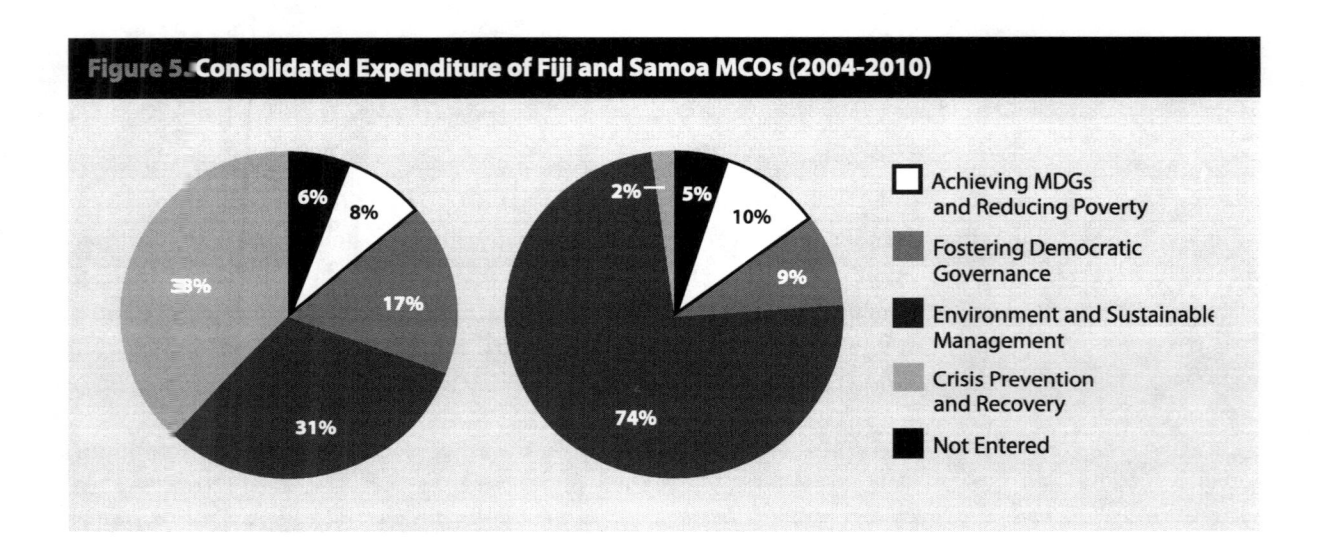

Figure 5. Consolidated Expenditure of Fiji and Samoa MCOs (2004-2010)

- Samoa MCO top two priorities based on value of allocated budget and expenditures were in Outcome 3 – Environment Sustainable Management (74 percent) and Outcome 1 – Achieving MDGs and Reducing Poverty (10 percent).
- Country-level resources sourced from core and non-core funding are governed and allocated through the CPAP. An overview of country-specific budget and expenditure covered under the Fiji and Samoa MCO between 2004 and 2010 are highlighted in Tables 7 and 8.

The PICs that received funding from the MCOs during this period did not spend more than the allocated budget. This was attributed mainly to the fluctuating rate of disbursement from year to year. The main reasons for the fluctuations in yearly disbursements were the dynamic

Table 7. Programme Budget and Expenditure by Fiji MCO (2004-2010, US$ Thousands)

Practice Area	Fiji Budget	Fiji Expenditure	Micronesia Budget	Micronesia Expenditure	Kiribati Budget	Kiribati Expenditure	Marshall Islands Budget	Marshall Islands Expenditure	Nauru Budget	Nauru Expenditure
Achieving MDGs and Reducing Poverty	2,241	1,694	316	217	720	369	1,227	619	660	511
Fostering Democratic Governance	11,950	8,418	145	83	1,804	1,411	781	516	394	236
Environment and Energy for Sustainable Development	22,063	15,296	1,753	1,028	1,982	1,298	1,056	723	895	651
Crisis Prevention and Recovery	181	93	0	0	0	0	0	0	0	0
Not entered	5,406	3,618	167	117	512	364	229	80	48	24
Total	41,841	29,119	2,381	1,445	5,018	3,442	3,293	1,938	1,997	1,422

Practice Area	Palau Budget	Palau Expenditure	Solomon Islands Budget	Solomon Islands Expenditure	Tonga Budget	Tonga Expenditure	Tuvalu Budget	Tuvalu Expenditure	Vanuatu Budget	Vanuatu Expenditure
Achieving MDGs and Reducing Poverty	684	265	5,766	4,169	634	362	1,438	964	3,365	2,192
Fostering Democratic Governance	210	103	11,491	8,196	261	171	1,157	880	911	694
Environment and Energy for Sustainable Development	1,144	669	2,421	1,321	1,530	994	2,084	1,375	1,971	1,507
Crisis Prevention and Recovery	0	0	7,030	4,005	398	143	0	0	0	0
Not entered	235	125	986	310	114	40	169	77	931	433
Total	2,273	1,162	27,694	18,001	2,937	1,710	4,848	3,296	7,178	4,826

Source: UNDP Fiji MCO, 2011

Table 8. Programme Budget and Expenditure by Samoa MCO (2004-2010, US$ Thousands)

Practice Area	Samoa Budget	Samoa Expenditure	Cook Islands Budget	Cook Islands Expenditure	Niue Budget	Niue Expenditure	Tokelau Budget	Tokelau Expenditure
Achieving MDGs and Reducing Poverty	4,327	2,332	75	0	123	58	233	190
Fostering Democratic Governance	2,572	1,832	255	135	495	289	320	97
Environment and Energy for Sustainable Development	27,843	17,846	654	425	1,019	605	1,212	502
Not entered	2,848	1,122	380	156	93	50	110	3
Total	38,376	23,690	1,364	716	1,750	1,006	1,963	797

Source: UNDP Samoa MCO, 2011

nature of government reforms and priorities, the PICs' ability to manage and disburse funds effectively and also their ability to secure additional resources from alternative development partners for the identified priorities.

The absorptive capacities of the MCOs were also flagged as an ongoing challenge and critical to ensure effective administration and monitoring of country programmes. The human resource base for the Samoa MCO has a total approved strength of 25 posts, of which 13 are funded by extra-budgetary resources. The staffing budget for 2011 is US$1,195,000 of which 55 percent is non-core funded. The Fiji MCO has 52 posts of which 28 posts are funded by extra-budgetary resources. Of the total funding of $3,256,995 for staffing, 25 percent is funded by extra-budgetary resources. The Pacific Centre has a total staffing of 37, with a total staffing budget of $3,900,000. The sub-office in Solomon has a total administrative budget of $249,900. The Country Presence Office costs are shared among UNDP, UNFPA and UNICEF with each office having a lead agency. The average UNDP cost of a Joint Presence Office is US$51,000.

It is pertinent to mention here that both MCOs operate under certain constraints in their business processes, which is not the case in most other country offices of UNDP. The two MCOs operate in an environment where financial transactions/transfers are carried out in multi-currency modes. There are six different currencies in operation. The banking systems vary from underdeveloped to undeveloped in many of the countries. The geographical distance make procurements more complex and CIF values are higher in many cases than standard UN agreed prices. In a NEX and NIM modality in the subregion, these constraints potentially impact on efficiency.

The geographical disadvantages, added transaction and financial costs of operating in a vastly spread subregion, and the complexities of business processes stated above require some special considerations in terms human resources and operating budgets.

Chapter 4
CONTRIBUTION OF UNDP TO DEVELOPMENT RESULTS

This chapter follows the four thematic outcome focuses of the UNDP Multi-Country Programmes. Within these themes, the eight outcomes elaborated in the results framework are examined. In addition, gender equality and capacity development remain as important cross-cutting elements of UNDP work, which will be separately elaborated on in Chapter 5.

Each outcome area will start with a short context and rationale consistent with regional context and development issues elaborated in Chapter 2. For illustrative purposes, assessment on key related project interventions from different countries will be presented using the different evaluation criteria, to the extent applicable, under country headings. The purpose of this section is not to illustrate all outputs of all projects but to assess the contribution to agreed outcomes.

4.1 OUTCOME 1. POVERTY REDUCTION AND THE MILLENNIUM DEVELOPMENT GOALS

4.1.1 CONTEXT

The global economic and financial crises have adversely impacted on the Pacific region, reversed progress made in some countries, hindered progress towards the achievements of MDGs in many others and slowed down progress in few countries that still managed to stay on-track. The Pacific region as a whole is unlikely to achieve all targets for poverty, employment and gender by 2015, as approximately 25 percent of households in the region live under the basic-needs poverty line. Despite moderate improvements, Pacific island states face tremendous challenges.

Pacific island leaders and governments have endorsed and embraced the relevance and utility of the MDG framework noting that it would be most useful in focusing and improving the integration of policy, planning and budgeting into national sustainable development strategies, and in monitoring progress. Adapting the goals through specific targets and indicators to more accurately reflect regional, national and sub-national contexts and priorities can facilitate more meaningful and useful assessment of poverty-reduction efforts as well as of development performance in general. All Pacific countries have committed themselves to achieve the MDGs and most governments have taken ownership by internalizing or localizing the MDGs with some specific national goals and targets.

Currently, nearly all countries in the region have integrated or are in the process of integrating the MDGs into their national development processes and many have reported on progress. All countries have plans for continued advocacy, monitoring and reporting, and implementation. Thus, at the two-thirds point between the Millennium Summit (2000) and the deadline to reach the MDGs (2015), there is wide acceptance and understanding of the MDGs as a useful development framework to address economic, social and ecological challenges.

Despite this progress, PICs face numerous challenges in their efforts to systematically target and reduce growing poverty and hardship through national planning and development frameworks. There is a clear need for accurate and timely macro-economic and poverty data and analysis on which to base poverty-reduction strategies or institute pro-poor policy reform; and further demonstration of how costing sectoral priorities can inform policy strategies and resource allocation decisions to achieve the MDGs. There is also a pressing need for improved capacity in generating, analysing and utilizing quality data and information on poverty in order to better target interventions to the most vulnerable populations and areas. Also needed is strengthened institutional capacity for monitoring national development plans, stronger links between national/sectoral planning and budget processes and the review and monitoring of these processes, and improved coordination among donors, regional organizations and UN agencies in providing support to countries.

Achievement of MDGs would require accelerated measures through national strategies with necessary budgetary allocations. The focus would be interventions such as programmes to generate employment while improving infrastructure, food security, enhancing provision of adequate social services including social protection, reducing household costs for education and health, trade liberalization, small and medium-sized enterprise promotion, vocational and technical training and entrepreneurial skills development, promoting financial inclusion, and reducing persistent social gaps. A greater commitment is required to create an environment that is genuinely supportive of private-sector investment and employment creation. These interventions, however, need to be anchored in national development strategies with adequate budgetary allocations, appropriate governance institutions, policy frameworks, and robust publics-sector institutional capacity.

4.1.2 UNDP STRATEGY

To support the emerging national efforts in above areas, UNDP's strategic thrust under this thematic outcome in the CPDs 2003-2007 and 2008-2012, was to assist the PICs in developing and implementing evidence-based and inclusive National Sustainable Development Strategies (NSDS) to stimulate economic growth, facilitate globalization and promote sustainable livelihoods. To help achieve this outcome, UNDP MCPD (Fiji MCO) outlined interventions in the PICs in following areas: (a) formulation and implementation of national and sectoral plans and strategies aligned with MDGs, targets and indicators and clearly linked to national budgets, (b) strengthened national statistical systems to focusing on poverty indicators (c) improving aid management systems linking to national plans and budgets; (d) facilitation of inclusive and equitable trade mechanisms, private-sector partnerships, employment generation policies and enhancing financial competencies; and (e) formulation of evidence-based and inclusive action on HIV and AIDS.

4.1.3 ASSESSMENT

SAMOA

MDG Acceleration programme: Samoa is preparing for a transition from LDC to Middle Income Country (MIC) status by January 2014. Prompted by the need to identify and cultivate new policy directions and pathways towards achieving the MDGs, the Government decided to consolidate all existing and planned UNDP-supported initiatives on pro-poor policy analysis, MDG reporting, and trade into an overall integrated framework for the acceleration of MDG achievement. This MDG Acceleration programme would target macro policy levels while drawing on the positive lessons learned from existing projects and programmes at the community levels and best practices from around the world. The overall objective is to inform the policy-makers with a full range of high-quality policy options and enable the government to focus its efforts in areas of greatest impact in reducing poverty and attaining a higher level of human development.

UNDP has been active over the years in Samoa in bringing the MDGs into the planning process, and continually promoting pro-poor policies. UNDP supported the Household Income and Expenditure Study (HIES) in Samoa, which has provided important and reliable data for planning at all levels. In addition, it carried out a poverty analysis of the data in cooperation with the Samoa Bureau of Statistics.

A separate analysis was carried out on the requirements for industrial growth, an important factor in achieving the goal of 'eradicating extreme poverty and hunger'. This analytical report has provided important guidance and input to the forthcoming national and sectoral plans for 2012-2015 in Samoa. It assessed policy options for economic growth in terms of strengths, weakness, and earlier actions and proposed key policy options that could shift current economic trends by leveraging existing strengths and minimizing constraints in order to create more inclusive growth processes and reduce poverty. It concluded that an effective industrial strategy for Samoa requires a reversal of the long-term decline of farming, and a strong focus on specific intersectional linkages between natural resources and value-added products, and services to increase competitiveness.

Pro-poor policy options studies: Under this stream, UNDP is conducting comprehensive policy analysis to identify feasible policy options to address the gaps identified in the MDG report, particularly slow economic growth and rising poverty and unemployment, and accelerate progress towards the achievement of MDGs. This exercise is to guide the national, provincial and sectoral plans to promote inclusive growth, job creation, and poverty reduction and to provide policy-makers with concrete and applicable pro-poor policy options and scenarios.

This is an ongoing initiative and the key policy areas being covered include:

- fiscal policies
- industry and manufacturing
- tourism
- agriculture and fisheries
- labour policy
- social policy
- monetary and financial systems
- banking systems

The Integrated Framework for Trade-related Technical Assistance: The key output of the project is the development, implementation and integration in national policies of a Diagnostic Trade Integration Study (DTIS) and accompanying action matrix. UNDP supported this process so that the Government could access further support from the Extended Integrated Framework (EIF) in Geneva to face the challenges of integration into the World Trade Organization (WTO).

The Private Sector Support Facility (PSSF): The PSSF was developed to support environmentally sustainable and gender-sensitive development led by the private sector through small grants to private businesses. The PSSF was designed to harmonize donor support to enable the Government to support the strengthening of local businesses targeting private-sector development particularly of small and medium-sized enterprises in the rural areas where most hardship is experienced. While both of the above projects proposed to promote gender equality, there are no provisions to do so, and women are a minority of fund recipients. Similarly, gender was almost entirely absent from the DTIS.

Assessment: The Government in various interactions confirmed that effectiveness in UNDP core-funded projects is helping to move issues and processes forward. UNDP's systematic technical inputs are considered of a high quality in their focus areas. Technical deliberations under different streams of the project raised more awareness on standards and best practices, and it provides useful inputs for the Government's planning and budgeting. The Accelerated MDG project is helping the Government to review macro policies in different areas and assess whether they are pro-poor. A comprehensive review exercise of the country's policy framework has already started under the project. This will be a significant contribution in infusing positive pro-poor dimensions in the country's policies. The Government is prepared to review and adjust policies as required once it is convinced by technical analysis of project work that some policies do not encompass necessary pro-poor dimensions. This mindset and preparedness certainly speak of the value of policy work carried out by UNDP.

The policy work supported by the advocacy work of UNDP has brought about an easy acceptance by the Government on the emerging poverty in Samoa. UNDP-assisted poverty study and household income survey were critical in revealing this phenomenon. The most recent household survey (2009) and the poverty analysis established that the percentage of people living below the poverty line has increased to 27 percent in 2010 from 15 percent a decade ago. This raised awareness of the intensity of the issue and initiated a dynamic within the policy thinking of the Government. The technical support and inputs by UNDP were vetted by the Government to be of excellent quality, timely and satisfactory. Samoa 2010 MDG Progress Report was also launched.

VANUATU

In Vanuatu UNDP interventions under this outcome consisted of three projects. The Localizing MDGs project is geared towards strengthening MDG-based planning, statistical and aid management systems. This is expected to facilitate evidence-based policy-making and planning by building upon existing mechanisms to ensure that reliable development data is available for decision-making. UNDP supported the strengthening of national development monitoring effort to collect MDG data as the basis for developing a national poverty line and preparing the second national MDG report by 2010. Discussions and review of documents revealed that the government has taken concrete steps for integration of MDGs into the planning and policy documents. MDG costing tools were introduced in workshops for government groups and civil society organizations to cost the different elements of the national plan as a basis for seeking budgetary allocation. The 2010 MDG Report was published and widely distributed.

The Integrated Framework Facility for Trade-Related Technical Assistance project is addressing the UNDAF objective of equitable growth and inclusive globalization. This is assisting the Government with initiating and implementing trade facilitation capacity development. The report on 'Integrated Framework for Trade' had been completed and validated by stakeholders in national workshops. The project has led to the incorporation of the DTIS Action Matrix into the Vanuatu National Development Strategy (PAA), which focuses on preparatory activities to facilitate WTO accession for Vanuatu. The project has led to strengthening of the Department of Trade with the capacity building of the Trade Unit to better negotiate WTO accession. It has also assisted with the review of customs legislation by the Customs Department and support for the Ministry of Trade and Ni Vanuatu Business. The Pacific Financial Inclusion Programme, a UNDP/UNCDF regional project, has also closely complemented the activities of the Integrated Framework for Trade with the improvement of financial literacy/competency of communities and facilitating action and investments by private sector to extend services to the 'unbanked' segment of the rural communities.

In the Facilitating HIV/AIDS-related Policies and Leadership Development project, UNDP is supporting the national sector-wide planning process and the development of national leadership. It will also focus on MDG 6 (HIV/AIDS) by supporting the traditional, religious, community, political and civil society leadership.

Assessment: The Localization of the MDGs Initiative project has contributed to mainstreaming the MDGs in the planning and budgeting processes. The 2010 MDG report has been published and MDG costing tool training has been introduced. There is general awareness and understanding of the MDGs not only within the central policy and planning agencies but also in the key line Ministries like Education and Agriculture. The real challenge is building and holding capacity to take the MDG mainstreaming to next level of having a fully costed MDG plan which could be closely linked to the annual budgeting systems. The mid-term review of the Priorities and Action Agenda (PAA) undertaken in 2011 saw the successful integration of MDGs as part of the monitoring and evaluation framework of the PAA. The Vanuatu Government led by the Department of Strategic Policy, Planning and Aid Coordination, has produced consecutive Annual Development Reports on the progress of the implementation of the national development priorities as expressed in the PAA and the Planning Long and Acting Short (PLAS) matrix. Progress on MDG targets and indicators are included in the ADR and, in this regard, has been a milestone in terms of promoting local ownership and accountability using national resources for the achievement of MDGs.

The Integrated Trade Framework Facility project, through its outputs, has led to the strengthening of the customs legislation, capacity building of the Trade Department and focusing on improving accessibility of the cooperatives to rural financial services. The Department of Cooperatives and Ni Vanuatu Business claim that there has been a significant increase in the savings of the cooperatives as a result of the project's targeted support for the cooperatives to access financial services. Related to this output are the financial inclusion programme activities which have led to the partnership of Digicel and National Bank of Vanuatu in introducing mobile phone banking to cover the provincial areas covered by the Digicel network. Effectiveness of the activities linked to improving financial literacy of the provincial cooperatives could have been further enhanced if there was close coordination at the formulation and implementation stages of the Integrated Framework for Trade and the Financial Inclusion Programme.

COOK ISLANDS (CKI)

In the Samoa MCPD 2003-2007, UNDP support focused on three areas: economic and social policies and strategies focused on the reduction of poverty, particularly through information and communication technology (ICT); creating an enabling environment for sustainable human development working at sub-national levels, and; sustainable management of natural resources, incorporating global environmental concerns and commitments. In the current CPAP for Cook Islands, UNDP has focused on: equitable economic development and poverty reduction by addressing MDG 1 (eradicating poverty) and MDG 3 (promoting gender equality) through a series of activities focused on gender-sensitive planning, and support to monitoring MDGs.

Cook Islands is a reasonably wealthy country but hardships are caused primarily by the high cost of living in the main island, and the high cost of transportation in the outer islands. UNDP has supported the CKI Government in developing its MDG monitoring capacity and incorporating MDGs into national planning. This has been accomplished, in the current CPAP, through the provision of a high-level local consultant to work in the Planning Department of the Prime Minister's Office, training (a small number) of planning staff, assessment of implementation of the current (2007-2010) plan and support to identifying sources of information for monitoring and production of the 2009 MDG report. The resulting report contains a thorough analysis of MDG accomplishments and shortcomings that also integrates a gender perspective. The two areas where CKI is weakest are environmental sustainability and governance. As the new development plan remains to be approved and published, it is not yet known how comprehensively it will include the MDGs.

According to the Annual Poverty Thematic Trust Fund (PTTF) reports for 2009 and 2010, MDG planning and budget support workshop was held in Cook Islands with participation of all the four islands. Subsequently, strategic planners were integrated into planning department in CKI. In CKI the project accomplishments include production and policy discussion on two documents:

- 'Te Kaveinga Nui': National Sustainable Development Plan, Monitoring and Evaluation Summary Report, December 2008. This was the first document to monitor the progress of the National Sustainable Development Plan (NSDP) 2007-2010.

- National Millennium Goals Report 2010 was a comprehensive analysis of where CKI stands in relation to the achievement of its MDG commitments. It is separate from the above report which did not reflect MDGs, since these were not integrated into the NSDP.

The project enabled the Planning Office of the Prime Minister's Office to identify and systematize the kinds of information and sources needed for monitoring the MDGs in the future. These have now been incorporated into the planning processes and will be reflected in the next national development plan, which is still in the process of approval. The project also carried out an in-house assessment of the planning capacity and provided necessary training to two other planners in the department. Incidentally, both subsequently left the Planning Department, taking their skills to other government departments. As a result of the orientation and activities of the project, the planning process of the upcoming national plan has been much more participatory, particularly for the outer islands whose participation was limited in the past. Previously consultation had involved only local officials and not community members.

The final outcome can be assessed when the new Sustainable National Development Plan is released. It is expected to incorporate MDG goals, strategies to achieve them, budgets to carry them out and monitoring tools to assess the outcomes. Important lessons learned from the experience included the need to link national plans with sector plans and for better budgeting processes at the level of various ministries. Human resources are a major issue in the smaller island countries like CKI. A single strategically selected and placed individual can have very high impact. With high-level international mobility, capacity development is a gamble. However, if the human resources circulate within the government, there is still a net gain. The major weakness in meeting MDG goals in CKI is mainly in the area of governance and environmental sustainability. Addressing these areas are the most likely ways to ensure poverty and sustainable livelihoods.

KIRIBATI

The current programme cycle seeks to support Kiribati's Development Plan (KDP) 2008-2011 and to strengthen its linkages with the Pacific Plan. The current programme includes 'Poverty Reduction and the Millennium Development Goals (MDGs)' as one of the key strategic outcome area.

The project on Localizing MDGs (strengthening MDG-based planning, statistical and aid management systems) included preparation of the MDG Report for 2008, support for completion of the KDP 2008-2011, aid management scoping and completion of poverty analysis report. (Ministry of Finance, Department of Statistics and Department of National Planning)

The project on strengthening MDG-based planning, statistical and aid management systems was completed in 2008 with the publication of the KSDP 2008-2011. The project made notable contribution in supporting the processes and making substantive inputs in the formulation of KSDP and MDG report. The 2008 MDG report was also completed alongside the KSDP. The outputs of scoping of aid management and poverty analysis were also delivered within the time-frame. The project process helped to generate the local capacity for such analytical work. This contributed heavily in enabling the Government of Kiribati taking on the lead for the preparation of the KDP 2012-1015 (with funding support from AusAID). The national execution modality used was seen as appropriate for timely and effective recruitment of appropriate local experts.

The objective of the Integrated Framework Facility for Trade-Related TA to LDCs (Ministry of Commerce Industry and Cooperatives) project was to ensure that trade is fully mainstreamed into the national planning and policy documents based on pro-poor strategies. The main outputs to be delivered were the completion of the DTIS report, national validation workshop and the technical submissions for the EIF. The DTIS report had been completed and endorsed by a national validation workshop. However, the financial proposals for seeking assistance to address the bottlenecks identified in the report have yet to be submitted to the EIF due to the delays encountered in the formal endorsement of the report by the Government.

TONGA

In the 2008-2012 CPAP, UNDP interventions included the following areas of support:

- Strengthening MDG planning to facilitate evidence-based planning: this involved strengthening national MDG monitoring capacity, ensuring use of data for developing national poverty line and ensuring production of a 2010 MDG report.

- MDGs have been incorporated into the Tonga Strategic Planning Framework including the 2011 Budget address.

- Efforts are ongoing to mainstream the MDGs into Government Department corporate plans.

Support to poverty reduction and the MDGs: The second National MDG report was published in September of 2010 and officially launched early in 2011. The project trained government statisticians and planners in monitoring and budgeting for MDGs. MDGs have been incorporated into the Tonga Strategic Planning Framework, including the 2011 Budget address. Efforts are ongoing to mainstream the MDGs into government department corporate plans. However, they are already referred to in other government planning documents, such as the Social Protection Issues Paper produced by the Ministry of Finance and Planning. There is a high level of awareness in the Government of the MDGs, and a campaign underway to make them widely known throughout the country. MDGs appear to be having an important impact on government policy: in the Ministry of Education, for example, the MDGs have increased awareness of needs of outer island schools.

Tonga has included the international indicator for poverty (under $1.25 a day), which is to be halved from 4 percent in 2004 to 2 percent as the target. More usefully it also tracks the proportion of people living below the national poverty line (16.2 percent in 2001) and the national poverty gap. Tonga has also adopted its own national target[32] for women in parliament - 2. The current parliament has 17 elected seats available to any adult man or woman, nine reserved for nobles who are all male, and up to four men or women who can be appointed by the king. Currently there is one woman legislator, appointed by the king.

Part of the poverty reduction strategy of UNDP in Tonga was the development of a national retirement scheme. This was in recognition partly of the growing number of elderly who are currently supported by family and remittances but may not be so in the future, as families become increasingly nuclear and their resources come under pressure.

The Government is committed to achieving the MDGs and owns the process, partly through adopting its own indicators. MDGs are specifically referred to in other projects such as SLM; used as a basis for vulnerability study by the Ministry of Finance and Planning; integrated into the education programme, especially water, sanitation and hygiene provisions in the outer islands, and in issues of nutrition and health nationwide in response to non-communicable diseases issues, where the MDGs are lagging.

SOLOMON ISLANDS

The two projects under this outcome area, Support to Aid Coordination and MDG Initiative, were developed based on the priorities identified by the Government and elaborated in the CPAP. They are fully aligned with the national priorities.

The MDGs are fully integrated in to the SOI Medium Term Development Strategy (MTDS) both as goals and targets as well as performance-monitoring indicators. By all evidence, the SOI

---

32 UNDP, 'Tonga MDG Assessment Survey 2010' 2010.

progress towards achievement of MDG goals is slow and the per capita income remains the lowest in the region. The weak record of national economic performance and the achievement of MDGs can to a large extent be attributed to weak national capacities. The weak capacities also impacted on the quality of the development planning processes, causing under resourced strategies and budgets with consequential impact on implementation at the people's level. The combinations of weaknesses of planning, monitoring and implementation processes coupled with weak human resource capacity impinge strongly on achievement of MDG targets. Hence, the need for focused support for MDG national initiatives.

Likewise, aid coordination has been an area of priority for the MDTS. Weak institutional processes and lack of adequate skilled capacity constrain effective aid coordination within the government. The CPAP proposed that the activities in the outcome area of 'equitable economic growth and the MDG programme' will be geared towards strengthening MDG-based planning awareness, and strengthening of aid coordination and aid management systems.

Both these programmes were formulated after proper consultation with the ministry and full consideration was given in reflecting the needs and aspirations of the MTDP. In this context, both projects were considered very timely and relevant.

In the implementation process, the MDG project seems not to have engaged the ministry in the process activities. There was a clear sense of indifference to ownership of the project by the relevant people in the ministry. The ministry felt that the project activities were driven in an isolated fashion without due engagement and involvement of all the relevant professional of the ministry. The perception was that the project was following UNDP's own requirements. The ministry officials met indicated that they had no accurate sense of the progress towards the achievement of the objectives of the project. Hence there were no details available from the ministry officials on actual outputs or contribution to outcomes.

The aid coordination project is driven by the ministry and the activities were fully integrated into the work stream of the ministry. The project was meeting the priority requirements of the ministry in the area of aid coordination. The project results, however, are not moving at the required pace. It suffered from substantial implementation delay due to delays in fielding experts. The implementation efficiency of UNDP had an impact on the pace of the delivery of outputs. Out of the four components only 'aid data system management' is progressing well as it was prioritized for action and there was substantial demand for it by the development partners and donors. The major component of developing an aid management system is yet to gain momentum. The ministry felt the need to gear up activities and steps need to be taken to expedite the unimplemented components – possibly alternative implementation options such as intermittent technical support from a qualified consultant or institutional outfit, if availability of longer term expertise is causing the delay. At the current pace, the delivery of results would require a much longer time than anticipated.

The results in this outcome area are clearly faced with efficiency issues. The reaping of development results is contingent upon full-fledged implementation of all components of both projects. The capacity development part needs more concerted and focused attention both from the Government and UNDP. Hence the sustainability element in both projects seems unlikely. But the Government seemed to be keen to go the extra step to designate people for process and technical training in aid coordination, making it a good candidate for a technical monitoring mission for implementation review, quality assurance of its technical work and the establishment of a more dynamic approach.

Both the projects are filling an important void in view of the need to generate adequate planning and implementation processes within the Government. The very large aid component in the development expenditure and the inadequacy of the Government's systems, processes and capacities to manage the flow and direction of resources to priority areas make the projects even more relevant. The counterfactual question was addressed by the Government stating that UNDP is the only assistance provider in this area and without the project the scenario will certainly look much worse.

Overall Assessment: UNDP's programme focus on poverty reduction and MDGs is of immediate strategic relevance to the needs of the PICs. Poverty has emerged as a significant and growing issue for most PICs. The national statistics display growing disparities in income, opportunities and well-being between rural and urban dwellers, and a growing underclass of landless, urban poor. Inability on the part of Pacific island economies to generate enough formal and informal sector jobs and livelihood opportunities has been contributing to the rise in poverty and income inequality as well as to 'poverty of opportunity'. As such, Pacific island governments have recognized poverty as a concept relevant to the Pacific that needs to be addressed through pro-poor policies and good governance. The Pacific subregion also continues to live through the adverse impact of the global economic and financial crises. This has reversed or slowed down progress in many countries.

Recognizing that the MDG framework would be the most useful vehicle in focusing and improving the integration of policy, planning and budgeting into national sustainable development strategies, all Pacific countries have committed themselves to achieve the MDGs and have taken ownership by internalizing or localizing the MDGs. In this context, UNDP's focus on poverty and supporting national efforts of achieving MDGs is highly relevant, timely and proving to be effective in facilitating national efforts. The activities under outcome 1 above includes substantial number of project and non-project initiatives of UNDP focusing on poverty analysis, developing poverty strategy and mainstreaming MDGs in the national context. Specific MDG- and poverty-related support was provided to Samoa, Vanuatu, Kiribati, Solomon Islands, Tonga, Cook Islands, Nauru, Fiji and Tokelau, Palau and Marshall Islands.

4.2 OUTCOME 2. GOVERNANCE AND HUMAN RIGHTS

4.2.1 CONTEXT

The PICs aim to achieve sustainable and equitable economic growth and poverty reduction in the medium term. But this achievement will significantly depend on the pace and magnitude of governance reforms and improvements. Alleged abuse of power, corruption and cronyism in some countries have contributed to instability and conflict, and a failure to uphold human rights, constraining economic growth and social progress. Accountability institutions are weak, poorly functioning and often lack capacity or resources.

There are good reform initiatives on decentralization and participatory decision-making in small atoll countries through the Strengthening Decentralized Governance project in Kiribati (SDGIK), through the Strengthening Local Governance project phase II (SLG II) in Tuvalu and through the Provincial Government Strengthening Programme (PGSP) in Solomon Islands. Mechanisms to encourage full and real participation by women and minority groups are still largely lacking. Local government and outer island planning and management could be enhanced through leveraging information and communication technology (ICT). But this requires initiative and support from the public sector.

The PICs increasingly recognize the value of broad-based civic education programmes. The perception of role of civil society organizations (CSOs) are also changing. They are increasingly recognized as potential key partners by governments and donors in governance and human rights education. Although key human rights conventions have been ratified by many PICs, the reporting on violations and progress towards fulfilling those commitments remains as a major shortcoming. All PICs (except Palau and Tonga) have ratified CEDAW and have national plans of action to promote gender equality and strategies to address gender-based violence. Yet legal and institutional mechanisms have not been developed or legislated in most to implement them.

For the Pacific island countries the 2008-2012 UNDAF outcome 2 for good governance focuses on "national and regional governance systems exercise the principles of inclusive good governance, respecting and upholding human rights; and resilient Pacific island communities participate in decision-making at all levels". The governance focus is centred on the parameters of the Pacific Islands Forum Pacific Plan. Of the 14 Pacific island countries assessed by the ADR, 13 are member states, except for Tokelau, which has an observer status.

The UNDP MCPD (2008-2012) focuses on the following two outcomes in the governance area:

1. Pacific island countries demonstrate and uphold the Forum Principles of Good Leadership and Accountability. The good leadership principles include respect for law and system of government; respect for cultural values, customs and traditions; respect for freedom of religion; respect for people on whose behalf leaders exercise power; respect for members of the public; economy and efficiency; diligence; national peace and security and respect for office. The principal accountability principles include a variety of compulsory provisions: a transparent budget process with full involvement of the Parliament/Congress; full audit of accounts of governments; open advertisement and competitive basis for public procurements; disciplinary action on contravention of financial regulations; auditor-general and ombudsman having independent reporting rights to Parliament/Congress; and the Central Bank with statutory responsibility for non-partisan monitoring and advice.

2. Pacific island countries have enhanced decentralization of governance and participatory decision-making.

UNDP interventions in specific countries through the country programme since 2004-2011 concentrated on supporting strengthening and reforming parliaments (Fiji, Solomon Islands, Palau, Kiribati, RMI, FSM, Vanuatu), constitutional reform (Nauru), supporting civic education (Fiji) and a broader support to local governance and decentralization through enhancing community participation, enhancing capacities of outer island communities, community profiling for facilitating service delivery, and developing and supporting institutional framework for decentralized governance (Solomon Islands, Tuvalu, Kiribati, Vanuatu, Cook Island).

The other stream of UNDP support to the countries was provided through the UNDP Pacific Centre. Its governance unit has been set up to provide policy advice in the form of country and regional research, and insights and knowledge on global good practices to the 14 PICs covered by the ADR.

The UNDP Pacific Centre rationalizes its focus on democratic governance as critical to the achievement of MDGs and is implementing the Governance in the Pacific (GovPac) project. This project focuses on the practice areas of parliament and associated legal frameworks and institutions (e.g., constitutional and electoral reform), accountability/anti-corruption, local governance, civil society, and justice and human rights.

For purposes of assessing development results in the governance outcome area and to have a better perception of UNDP's contribution, a country-based elaboration is presented below based on a sample of projects examined and available evidence.

4.2.2 ASSESSMENT

TUVALU

In the past two programme cycles, UNDP funded Support to Local Governance, phases I and II. An evaluation of the first phase was carried out in 2008 in order to contribute lessons learned for the 2008-2012 phase. It found that the programme was extremely relevant and recommended continuation, even though there were some limitations. The capacity of the Ministry of Home Affairs and Rural Development and Kaupule staff was strengthened as a result of improved capacity building interventions of the projects which were integrated with practical applications, linked to policy implementation and management and conducted on-site. Technical support was considered satisfactory, and the quality of projects proposed was improving. Among the improvements suggested for the next phase was upgrading in monitoring and evaluation, audit, research, and participatory plans in place of the current 'shopping list' approach to community development. Sustainability was raised as an issue, because all in-house experts are project based, and there was little interdepartmental coordination or synergies with other UNDP activities. In addition, the counterparts perceived that the response times by UNDP were often slow, delaying project implementation (often dependent on infrequent inter-island transportation) and financial flows.

It was felt by the Government that a milestone was the participatory approach to planning and budgeting (drafts are drawn up and consultations are held in all islands). The local budget has to be approved by the whole community (everyone over 18 can vote on it.) It was reported in the evaluation that this incorporated a small step to include women, and that some people felt empowered because they learned through the project that the traditional councils (falekaupule) were not the only source of authority: there were also national laws and local councils. On the other hand, the falekaupule felt the law confirmed their ultimate power, and therefore there were some conflicts. In addition, the falekaupule are generally all male and over 50 years of age, with traditional thinking, which does not recognize minority or women's rights, or freedom of religion. Of the 48 local council members elected throughout the islands, only two are women. Land is only inherited/owned by males in the family.

A major step in Tuvalu in the area of anti-corruption, was the endorsement by the Tuvalu Government's Departmental Coordinating Committee's proposal for ratification of the UN Convention Against Corruption (UNCAC) with a Cabinet paper. The next step is the endorsement by the cabinet for its ratification.

VANUATU

Project on Strengthening Parliament: In order to foster democratic and good governance practices in the country, UNDP, through the project, supported the Vanuatu Parliament's Corporate Plan. The project also included an induction workshop for Members of Parliament, enhancing the capacity of the Parliamentary secretariat.

The UNDP Pacific Centre, in collaboration with MCO Fiji, played a visible role in the revision of the leadership code and review of the office of the ombudsman, and commenting on the proposed amendment of the Ombudsman Office Act Amendment legislation. Although the final outcome of process is yet to be visible, this is a necessary first step, and provided credible basis for strengthening and systematizing the much-needed oversight function within the Government. Work of Transparency International with UNDP support in providing workshops for enhancing the general public awareness on governance issues was found to be very popular. UNDP's support in facilitating the approval of the bill on Vanuatu's accession to UNCAC in November 2010 was highly appreciated. The evaluation mission received positive feedback from senior politicians about the effectiveness of the UNDP initiatives and encouraged stepping up more project activities to ensure enhanced accountability standards relating to the maintenance of the national leadership codes.

Project on Building Resilient Communities supporting Strengthening Decentralized Governance: This involved UNDP's three-year programme Building Resilient Communities in two key provinces (Penama and Shefa). Through working with village/grassroots structures, women and youth groups, and the civil society at large, improvement and promotion of rural sustainable development, peace, safety and stability is ensured. Increasing access to ICT by communities in Shefa and Penama will enable their participation in discussions and actions that affect their lives, and promote better understanding, peace and stability.

The building of resilient communities led to the implementation of the governance and disaster risk management plan for Penama province and the community resource profiling in Shefa province. ICT was also introduced to support the provinces of Shefa and Penama to assist the communications with these provincial communities. Introduction of ICT at the community level did not work out properly, as standalone ICT solutions for community-based projects could not be supported due to lack of adaptation of ICT policies by the central government. While most of the project outputs were achieved, their sustainability was undermined due to turnover of project staff and local counterparts.

TONGA

An important Parliamentary support plan recently started (2011-2013) will help to strengthen the efficiency and effectiveness of Tonga's first democratically elected parliament. Outputs are aimed at very systemic and practical matters such as developing a corporate plan, handbooks for MPs, document and records management. Prior to this a Legislative Needs Assessment was conducted which provided the platform for initiating Parliament support projects. This project further strengthened the capacities of Members of Parliament in their oversight role in the newly elected government after peaceful and successful elections in 2010. A properly functioning and transparent Parliament is likely to be more effective and provide greater confidence to the population.

Although there has been some uneasiness in the relationship between the Government and NGOs, the Government now recognizes the important role that CSOs play, and the special relationship and access they have to the population. NGOs in the past have participated in projects with the Government (e.g., civic education) but have often felt they have had little say in the projects. Tonga has an active and vibrant civil society, represented by the umbrella group Civil Society Forum of Tonga (CSFT), founded in 2001 and representing approximately 60 CSOs across the country. The previous government was not as favourable to NGOs, and the CSFT had to lobby it persistently to get the unspent UNDP budget redirected towards its organization.

UNDP's Strengthening Civil Society (2004-2008) project helped the CSFT strengthen and consolidate itself as an organization, through providing training workshops for members, participating in MDG training for NGOs (in CKI), mapping the NGO sector nationally, strengthening volunteer participation of youth, and linking with regional NGO networks such as PIANGO. According to the CSFT, a critical factor for success of the project was that the funds were available directly to NGOs. The CSFT felt an exit strategy would have helped it transition after funding ended, but the continuity of the project was insured by NZ funding, which will end soon. The CSFT will participate in the new UNDP regional programme (Pacific Centre), Strengthening Capacities for Peace and Development.

TOKELAU

The strategic priorities of UNDP support for Tokelau focused on:

- Support to referendum on self-governance, increased accessibility to basic human rights information and access to mechanisms to claim them; and strengthened governance institutions based on good governance principles, awareness raising campaigns on HIV/AIDS, national gender-sensitive priorities, plans, programmes and capacities in place to strengthen commitment to action at all levels to affect behaviour changes that ensure cost-effective and efficient care, treatment and support, to ensure achievement of MDG 6 (Combating HIV/AIDS, Malaria and other diseases).

- The Constitutional Development project has been effective not only in developing the Modern House of Tokelau under which the government structure for the three traditional villages on each atoll was formed with the three elected faipule designated as the Ülu o Tokelau but also the implementation of the 2006 and 2007 national referendum to determine the preferred type of government the Tokelau people want. The project has also been effective in raising awareness among the General Fono Members and the young up-and-coming community leaders on the value of practicing principles and best practices of good governance.

REPUBLIC OF MARSHALL ISLANDS

The Support to Parliament project (Stage 2) reflected a real need to upgrade the services available to the clerk to the Parliament for training of staff, strengthening the oversight role of Parliament, the drafting of staff manual and the setting up of a library resource centre. The evaluation of the project confirmed most of these features are in place, which has strengthened Parliament in many respects.

Its committees like the Public Accounts Committee are meeting more often with adequate staff support to carry out its important role of overseeing the use of public funds. There are other aspects in process, such as the notion of Parliament Corporate Plans which, if successful, will be an innovative feature. The evaluation of the project noted that the RMI Parliament had a very stable tradition. It had followed its four-year terms without a break; it has not had a vote of no-confidence and neither has the country had a coup since its inception. There is evidence of a push from within the RMI for greater efficiency, and greater accountability running through the projects. There is also a concomitant sense of ownership that pervades these moves, which augur well for sustainability.

REPUBLIC OF PALAU

There had been a Legislative Needs Assessment in 2008. Following this, an orientation workshop was provided for legislators. A parliamentary library was set up with some emphasis on delivering of information through research, but the installation of the IT system with wireless internet was not done until February 2011. In addition, a support package is being delivered including training of support staff and provision of help to Senators and Congress members in understanding the budget and in working together on common issues in Parliament. The Parliament is therefore in a better position to deliver the required services to its members and to the community as required of it under the Constitution.

KIRIBATI

Strengthening Parliament and Improving Participatory Democracy by improving capacity of Parliamentarians to effectively discharge their duties and also promoting public awareness on the functions and relevance of Parliament to the communities. (Office of Speaker and Ministry of Internal and Social Affairs). Most the project outputs have been achieved including the revision to the rules of procedures which resulted in clarity of interpretation and more efficient flow of Parliamentary proceedings, completion of the corporate plan for 2010-2015, enhancing the online research capabilities of Parliamentarians, improving the public profile of Parliament with the launching of website, and publication of a newsletter. An induction programme for new Parliamentarians is also being planned.

Strengthening decentralized governance between Government and Island Councils. This project aimed at institutional strengthening and capacity building at the sub-national levels, i.e., Island and Urban Councils. The project focuses on strengthening governance of outer islands by educating people to make informed and constructive decisions on issues affecting development of their village or island.

The planned second phase of the project on strengthening decentralized governance between Government and Island Councils during 2008-2011 has not yet started. A project design document has yet to be developed. However, feedback during the country consultations gave a positive outcome of the first phase under the

2003-2007 country programme. Based on an earlier review and direct consultations during the country visit, it is assessed as relatively successful with the achievement of the outputs linked to the development of profiles for seven islands, revision of the Local Government Act governing the island councils, capacity building for island councils, partial improvement of ICT for connecting of islands, promotion of awareness on human rights at the island council level and development of monitoring and evaluation for the overall outer island development programme. However, the inability to complete the output for development of financing network plans restricted the usefulness and sustainability of the project.

The Kiribati Parliament Support project has recently been the most visible of the UNDP projects after the successful facilitation by the Pacific Centre of the mock Parliament for Women similar to the youth mock Parliament previously supported by the Commonwealth Secretariat as part of national efforts for involving the communities to learn more about the important legislative role of Parliament. Most of the project outputs have been achieved, including the publication of the Parliamentary Handbook (an induction programme for new Parliamentarians is also being planned), completion of the corporate plan for 2010-2015, enhancing the online research capabilities of Parliamentarians, improving the public profile of Parliament with the launching of website, publication of a newsletter, an open day for Parliament for plans and annual budgets.

Most of the outputs of the first phase of the project on Strengthening Decentralized Governance and Outer Island Councils have been achieved. However, the inability to achieve the critical outputs for finalizing development and funding frameworks and the strengthening and facilitation of partnerships of the island councils and CSOs have significantly restricted the ability of the project to achieve its medium-term outcomes.

FIJI

The two projects on civic education were on track and contributed extensively and intensively laying a foundation for potential gains in the future governance processes in Fiji. Phase I of the Fiji Parliament Support Project was completed in 2007. It was not possible to move into the second phase due to the current political condition. UNDP supported Fiji's Election in 2001 and that project closed the same year.

The National Initiative on Civic Education (NICE): This project facilitated civic education to the diverse communities of Fiji. The project worked with civil society organizations and other influential special interest groups in developing a community civic education curriculum and delivering information on pertinent national governance matters, advocating for democracy, human rights and democratic governance. The project contributed to creation of a stock of informed, responsible and active citizenry through the dissemination of information, the communication of advocacy skills, and awareness-raising among the adult population of Fiji of the principles and characteristics of democracy. It also improved the capacity of participating civil society organizations on the content of civic education and on the delivery of civic education programmes through a community civic education curriculum developed jointly by the project and the partner CSOs.

An evaluation[33] of the project conducted in 2010, commended the project for its significant achievements and concluded that the criticality and relevance of the civic education initiative remains as relevant or even more so now, as at the project's inception in 2006. The project was a 'first' on many levels, especially in terms of knowledge transfer, collaboration between diverse groups for a common purpose and inclusivity of marginalized groups. The development of the national civic education curriculum and the consequent outreach at a local level are important

---

33   UNDP and Government of Fiji, 'Final Evaluation of the National Initiative on Civic Education (NICE) Project', Suva, April 2011.

achievements. The project met a real need and has created a new level of awareness at the CSO and beneficiary level of issues related to participation and democratic governance.

The progress towards outcome was considerable: 68,000 people, or 13 percent of the voter population, were trained. In the forthcoming 2014 elections, there will be a better preparedness and ability of a large number of voters to exercise their rights and choose better. The conceptual understanding demonstrated by the participants on democracy, human rights, and constitution was something that could not be attained from any other source. The project activities had an extensive coverage from the central urban level to villages and the outer islands. The reason behind such a level of success is the direct involvement of the CSOs as implementers with their strong outreach and interface with the general population and specially the rural folks. Although observing the direct results in the short run seems inconceivable, the project investments in civic education created potential for future leverage.

The Fiji In-School Citizenship Education Project (CEP) was designed to facilitate the inclusion of human rights and civic values topics in both primary and secondary school curricula and support the teaching of such topics widely and thoroughly through their infusion into assessed or examinable subjects. The project supported the development of relevant citizenship education curricula; the production of related resources; the design, development and testing of instructional materials; the training of teachers; and the introduction of civics education into the formal school system.

A project evaluation conducted in early 2011 concluded the project has achieved its purpose of commencing compulsory teaching of a comprehensive human rights and civic education curricula at all levels in schools. It has contributed towards the goal of increased awareness of civic and human rights including the role of parliament, the rights of citizens and democratic processes in Fiji. The overall effects of the project on intended beneficiaries included: participation in a social learning process on citizenship education; improved teaching skills and approaches; increased tolerance and mutual understanding among learners; increased participation of students and parents in the teaching-learning process.

NAURU

Constitutional Reforms: The key objectives of the project were to complete a constitutional review process that is inclusive, open and reflects global democratic best practice. The ADR mission found that all the six steps of the constitutional reform process had been completed except for the milestone to secure the necessary support for the national referendum. It was noted that except for the provisions of the constitution needing the necessary minimum level of support by national referendum all other provisions of the constitutional reforms that have been passed as law by Parliament can now be legally effected. It will only require the redrafting of the text of the constitution to eliminate the cross references to the referendum-related draft provisions. The increase in public awareness and active public debate of constitutional issues relating to transfer of votes appear to be a product of past extensive public consultations during the constitutional reforms project.

Overall Assessment: Governance

Relevance: It is well known that policy and institutional constraints are at the heart of constraints to growth and poverty reduction in the Pacific. All the countries assessed have adopted the Pacific Plan objectives of "improved transparency, accountability, efficiency in management and use of resources in the Pacific". The PICs aim to achieve sustainable and equitable economic growth and poverty reduction in the medium term. Good robust governance is central to the achieving of the MDGs being pursued by the PICs.

UNDP interventions in specific countries through the country programme since 2004-2011 concentrated in supporting strengthening and reforming parliaments, constitutional reform, civic education and broader support to local governance and decentralization through enhancing community participation, capacities of outer island communities, facilitating service delivery, developing and supporting institutional framework for decentralized governance. UNDP programmes included initiatives and projects to support national policy capacities and governance systems to exercise the principles of inclusive, equitable, participatory, transparent and accountable governance and respect for human rights. The PICs' national efforts demonstrated priorities accorded to all these areas. UNDP governance thematic area projects as developed and implemented demonstrate strong relevance to these objectives.

The focus of the governance thematic area on strengthening of parliaments, and constitutional and electoral reforms are considered highly relevant in these relatively new independent countries, as the predominantly communal based traditional social and political structures are being moulded into centralized national government structures. Ownership of governance reforms at the national and community levels appears more pronounced for the relatively small island states as shown in the cases of Cook Islands, Tokelau, Nauru, Tuvalu and Kiribati. The support to decentralization and local governance is serving this aspiration through extensive project work at sub-national levels and outer islands.

The linkages of indicators identified in the monitoring and evaluation framework for the UNDAF 2008-2012 programme for the governance thematic interventions appear relatively weak. While UNDP interventions are mainly aimed at strengthening parliaments and supporting constitutional and electoral reforms the indicators being suggested for the monitoring and evaluation framework are centred on the broad global indices produced by the World Bank and Transparency International. This could partly explain why there has been relatively poor reporting also in the governance thematic area noted by the 2010 Pacific UNDAF midterm review 2008-2012. There is an urgent need to finalize and refine relevant indicators of the monitoring and evaluation framework for the UNDAF 2008-2012 if the governance programme is to be effectively monitored.

Effectiveness: The close alignment of key parameters of the UNDP country and regional governance programmes has been the main factor in generating the highly effective outputs of the country programme governance projects. These projects, in addition to the substantive programmatic monitoring by UNDP MCO, are also receiving added technical support of the UNDP Pacific Centre which contributed to quality of outputs. There is a growing recognition within the region that UNDP has now secured its competitive edge in governance reforms area. The current implementation arrangements combining the services of the MCO offices and the Pacific Centre for formulation, quality assurance and technical monitoring provides the professional edge required for quality work.

While there has been close coordination between UNDP and other regional development partners during the planning phase, there is very little evidence of this coordination continuing into the implementation phase. Effectiveness of the governance component on supporting the Pacific Islands Forum Principles of Good Leadership and Accountability, which was targeted mainly through the strengthening of parliaments, has been rated relatively successful as highlighted by the results of the parliamentary strengthening projects in Solomon Island, Kiribati and Nauru and Marshall Islands. There is opportunity for a more formal regional approach through the Pacific Centre for these parliamentary strengthening projects through which resources can be consolidated to provide support for the common activities like training for members of parliament and production of parliamentary manual particularly for those countries with similar models of government.

Effectiveness of the component on enhanced decentralization of governance and participatory decision-making has been limited due to the relatively more complicated designs of these types of projects for widely scattered and often geographically isolated islands/communities which need relatively long period of implementation to get some traction as shown in the cases of Cook Islands, Kiribati, Solomon Islands and Vanuatu.

Effectiveness of UNDP in advocating anti-corruption practices has picked up in the last 12 months with the accession of Vanuatu in July 2011 to the UN Convention against Corruption (UNCAC). Since then a number of other Pacific countries (Tuvalu and Solomon Islands) have started taking steps towards acceding to the UNCAC. This could be gauged by the highly active publicity campaign by the Pacific Centre since the accession of Vanuatu to the UNCAC.

The advocacy role of UNDP in human rights has had synergy with the governance and gender projects. The promotion of the mock parliament for women in Kiribati as part of the public-awareness component of the parliamentary strengthening project is a case in point. Effectiveness of the governance programme has been enhanced by the increasing practice of also including governance components for the community/island level projects, particularly in the environmental and sustainable management programme thematic area.

Efficiency: Resourcing for governance projects has been relatively successful particularly for the high-profile Parliamentary strengthening and constitutional reform projects. This has been further enhanced by the ability of UNDP to leverage its partnerships with the United Nations Democracy Fund (UNDEF). There is also evidence that the bilateral donors like AusAID and NZAID have also channelled funds to support governance project activities through UNDP projects in addition to their own governance projects.

Although there was negative feedback on the response time at the initial phases of planning the projects for parliamentary strengthening (Kiribati project manager appointment), constitutional (Nauru initial project design) reforms, UNDP response times to needs of Pacific island countries have been seen as becoming relatively fast with the UNDP Pacific Centre. The Centre has a team of professionals in the specialist areas of governance who have been able to provide alternative solutions. The active use of the internet in creating discussion groups who are briefed on a regular basis has also further enhanced this close connection of the Centre and their network of national counterparts. There are also online training courses now being promoted for anti-corruption and human development.

Although the Nauru constitutional reforms assignment could be considered as relatively efficient because of its relatively low overhead costs, the absence of a project management unit would have compromised the effectiveness of the project if the consultants had not put in long hours to keep the workflow moving. One of the main lessons learned from the Nauru constitutional reforms is that the design of these projects needs to incorporate appropriate costs of an administrative unit to support the team of consultants and also institute cash-flow arrangements to allow the flexibility for timely payments during the public consultations.

Sustainability: In both streams of governance projects (Strengthening Parliament and Support to Decentralization), there was evidence of efforts by governments in allocating human resources and institutional support (Vanuatu, Solomon Islands, Kiribati). However, the scale of support in some instances was not adequate. The long-term sustainability is ensured when outputs are internalized within national systems. In the parliament projects that was generally visible. But in the other areas such as decentralization it is too early to judge, although there was evidence of governments' strong support, budgetary outlay and institutional structure (Solomon Islands, Kiribati) which are essential preconditions of long-term sustainability. UNDP MCOs are supporting the sustainability of the governance projects by drawing on additional technical support through their in-house technical team of governance professional specialists in the Pacific Centre. The Centre is able to store institutional memory, continue ongoing relationships with the regional network of local counterparts and provide technical backstopping on demand.

Experience from the projects which targeted extensive involvement of the CSOs in civic education shows that sustainability of the project results is improved. This is particularly so where the CSOs have ownership of the project results as seen with the NICE project in Fiji and the Tonga Strengthening Civil Society project, which has helped in strengthening of the Civil Society Forum of Tonga (CSFT).

Incorporation of public education project activities into school curricula is seen as a one of the most effective ways for embedding the results and improving their sustainability, as shown in the Fijian example.

4.3 OUTCOME 3. CRISIS PREVENTION AND RECOVERY

4.3.1 CONTEXT

UNDP assistance in this area was aimed at strengthening the capacity of the PICs to prevent and manage crises and build resilience to the impact of tensions and disasters. Exposure to natural hazards such as volcanoes, tsunamis, cyclones, earthquakes (Solomon Islands and Vanuatu, which are among the most disaster-prone countries in the world) and experiences of civil unrest and conflict over the past decade (Fiji, Solomon Islands, Tonga and Vanuatu), have highlighted the need to focus more strongly on disaster risk reduction, peace and stability dialogues, early warning systems, and the role of women in crisis prevention and recovery. In the long term, it is increasingly recognized that democratic governance and poverty reduction are key in preventing potential conflicts.

Under this outcome, UNDP focused on formalizing institutional mechanisms for mainstreaming disaster risk reduction into national development and budgetary strategies (in Solomon Islands and Vanuatu); and development and implementation of national policies and plans addressing human security through conflict-sensitive analysis and tension reduction interventions (in Fiji, Marshall Islands, Tonga and Solomon Islands). This outcome was supported through projects providing (a) support to the development of an integrated approach to addressing and reducing vulnerability to tension and disaster; (b) effective recovery strategies that seek to build capacity to address the root causes of humanitarian crisis and natural disasters; and (c) addressing the long-term livelihood needs of communities.

UNDP demonstrated strong capacity in coordinating response to emergencies and natural disaster. UNDP's role in promptly responding and managing post-disaster response in Samoa, Tonga, Cook Islands and Solomon Islands were widely appreciated by the governments, the donors and affected communities. The interventions were considered timely and effective. In the case of the 2009 tsunami in Samoa, UNDP took a lead role in coordinating the donors in the rapid assessment and supporting the preparation for funding of the rehabilitation programme. It also coordinated the UN system support and leveraged all UN professional assistance from the Pacific region. Some country-level details are narrated below.

4.3.2 ASSESSMENT

FIJI

Following severe floods in the Western, Central and Northern Divisions of the Fiji Islands in January 2009, UNDP provided assistance to the Government through BCPR TRAC 3 funding of US$100,000. Through this project, an assessment of the capacity of Department of Agriculture to respond to and prepare for future disaster events was undertaken, and a disaster risk management strategy (DRM) was formulated for the agriculture sector to enhance the department's capacities. In parallel, a socio-economic assessment of the flood impact on households and private businesses in Ba, Central Division and Nadi was conducted between UNDP's Pacific Centre and the South Pacific Applied Geosciences Commission (SOPAC). Major areas assessed were structural damages, lost possessions and assets, medical costs, evacuation costs, relocation costs, lost wages and businesses, and reports cleared and endorsed by the Fiji Government for public viewing. During the project period in December 2009, Fiji was again hit by Cyclone Mick and, upon the Government's request, UNDP supported a rehabilitation programme to deliver plant cuttings, seedlings and weedicides to affected farmers, benefitting 7,578 families (approximately 30,312 people including men, women and children). This assisted in recovery and boosted agricultural production in low-lying and flood-prone areas, as well as contributed towards maintenance of a steady stream of products supplied to the markets and low-cost commodities for urban dwellers who rely on markets for their food.

The project was extended to December 2011 to allow for a workshop conducted by the Department of Agriculture to validate the DRM strategy formulated in October 2011. Through this strategy, an action plan to strengthen coordination within the department with relevant agencies was developed to prepare for and respond to future disasters in a more timely, coordinated and efficient manner. This involved regional actors such as OCHA and SOPAC and key relevant ministries including NDMO as well as civil society organizations (including NGOs and women's organizations).

TONGA

The principal activity in this practice area was support to early recovery, following the earthquake of 8.3 magnitude and three subsequent six-metre waves that traveled 600 metres inland in the northern island of Niuatoputapu. The disaster destroyed 90 percent of the houses in this low-lying island with a population of 1,665, killing nine and injuring many others.

UNDP was ready with an early recovery programme within two weeks of the disaster, although approval was delayed by a full month. A budget of US$300,000 was approved for the purposes of reactivating livelihoods among affected populations, and support strategic recovery planning to enhance disaster risk management systems. An island wide warning system (sirens) is in place, linked 24 hours a day to the meteorological centre in Tongatapu. However, plans to support a nationwide system were not implemented since the Government is planning its own.

Economic recovery involved replacement of lost fishing boats and nets; food for work in reconstruction projects, and tools (pots and sewing machines) for women's mat-weaving local industry. The weaving halls were completed in October 2011 and formally handed over to the community by UNDP. However, resettlement of affected women, men and children to safer grounds as planned by the Government and major donors has been delayed. According to Lands and Surveys, however, it has not yet been legally established who the buildings will belong to. Technical expertise was provided by the Pacific Centre, and the recovery plans designed were adopted by the Government of Tonga.

TOKELAU

Under the crisis prevention and recovery thematic area the Seawalls project was part of the programme. It not only involved the upgrading of existing seawalls and expanding new ones for Atafu, Nukunonu and Fakaofo atolls, but also the development of national and community-level disaster risk reduction and management plans. These plans have been effective in increasing community preparedness for natural disasters and in controlling coastal erosion, particularly during the cyclone seasons for the three atolls. The Community Centred Sustainable Development Project, focusing on crisis prevention and recovery, and development planning components have been effective. The Village Sustainable Development Plans for each of the three atolls in

Tokelau have been completed. However, the relatively high personnel turnover of a thin administrative pool of skills has restricted the effectiveness of this initiative at the community level.

SOLOMON ISLANDS

Truth and Reconciliation Commission (TRC): The project on TRC was considered most timely and relevant. It is an independent commission set up by an act of parliament and time-bound in it operation. The aftermath of the conflict required a process on independent investigation of the root causes of the tension and also due process investigations, seeking interview statements from the victims and other measures considered to bring closure to victim families. The relevance comes from the facts that:

- it is a mechanism to focus on human rights,
- it is seen as a continuation of the Ministry of National Unity, Reconciliation and Peace's work on peace-building since 2001,
- it is a means of dealing with outstanding issues by providing a mechanism for ordinary people.

The effectiveness and sustainability of the project in supporting the progress towards outcome has been noteworthy for the following reasons.

The ministry has developed a long-term action plan with clear follow-up on mental health policy waiting for approval of cabinet. The policy is comprehensive and recognizes addressing the trauma as a precondition for peace and development. The exhumation of remains of victims conducted through the project established the protocols of exhumation to incorporate the victims' community and cultural values. These brought closure to many victims' families and helped them move forward. The reparation helped the create space for victims. The scheme for rehabilitation of victims also helped resettlement. The process of the TRC works in itself as a contribution to the institutional reforms that the Government is initiating. The process of TRC contributed to a deep understanding of the root causes of the tension and conflict. The end of the project will be a good story to tell and that will be the most satisfying part of the project.

Efficiency: The efficiency aspect, according to the commissioners and the ministry, deserved improvement and attention, as the perception was that the design had an inefficient implementation mechanism. The delays in the recruitment process created an undue pressure on the effectiveness of TRC work as it had real time limits imposed by the Act. Many specific examples of administrative and management non-responsiveness were cited. The commissioners and the ministry highlighted the need for strengthening the implementation support capacity. Even the fast-track approach by UNDP seemed to not address the special needs and circumstances of the project. The efficiency impinged heavily on the progress towards outcome.

COOK ISLANDS (CKI)

Like most Pacific islands, CKI is vulnerable to natural disasters. In February 2010, Cyclone Pat hit CKI, causing massive damage in the island of Aitutaki. UNDP responded quickly to government requests for assistance with a one-year US$227,500 Early Recovery Project. Early recovery was facilitated by the rapid response of OCHA, UNDP, UNICEF and the Pacific Centre. Of particular value to the process was the expertise of a Disaster Risk Management expert from the UNDP Pacific Centre. In particular, taking a long-term view of recovery even in the early humanitarian stage of the disaster was a novelty whose value was eventually recognized and appreciated. It has influenced the way that other agents such as the local Red Cross and community groups approach emergencies. Less useful was the strategy to reactivate the economy, which in this case, was not severely damaged and reactivated itself quickly. Tourism, handicrafts and above-ground crops were back within nine months; rebuilding ('build back better' for housing) was financed by New Zealand and provided employment for men.

An important aspect of the emergency response was the involvement of the community, particularly through the Community Centred Sustainable Development Project, one of the UNDP projects supported through the environment/sustainable development practice area. In completing the Village Sustainable Development Plan, the local government and community organizations will be incorporating disaster risk management in the local plan. It was noted that the Community Centred Sustainable Development Project communities in Samoa played an important role in tsunami response and subsequent risk reduction.

The Emergency Management Cook Islands (EMCI) has extensive responsibility for developing disaster responses, ensuring that the private sector has DRR plans, training, developing awareness especially in the schools, and others. But, according to the Red Cross, the EMCI has only two staff members. The support of the international community in time of emergency is important, but more resources need to be put into the national mechanism.

4.4 OUTCOME 4. ENVIRONMENT AND SUSTAINABLE MANAGEMENT

4.4.1 CONTEXT

Heavy reliance on fragile land and in-shore marine environments characterize the Pacific economies and livelihoods. Sustainable development becomes an intense challenge in the face of acute increasing environmental risk and degradation. Population growth, urbanization, and an increased demand for cash income contribute to the emergence of localized environmental and natural resource management concerns. Climate change is a significant Pacific concern of global origin.

UNDP support in this arena is considered most relevant and timely. The support was provided through three streams of efforts: a) strengthened national capacity to develop and implement environmental policies, legislative and management frameworks and mainstreaming through national policies and budgets; b) strengthened capacities for improved access and management of multilateral environmental agreements; and c) sustainable livelihoods of vulnerable groups strengthened through institutional support and leveraging indigenous governance systems, to contribute to sustainable environmental management.

MCPDs (2008-2012) of Fiji and Samoa set the strategy of supporting a more resilient Pacific region by leveraging UNDP's global expertise and resources, and utilizing innovative approaches to strengthen capacity for sustainable management of environment and natural resources. The focus was placed on environmental governance, including promotion of sustainable renewable energy and adaptation to climate change into national strategies, as well as improving access to and management of multilateral environment agreements (MEAs). Programmatic activities were to further focus on partnerships and capacity development in order to strengthen the nexus among poverty reduction, sustainable environmental management and gender equity.

Country specific assessments of this outcome area are provided below following the evaluation criteria.

4.4.2 ASSESSMENT

VANUATU

Environmental protection and resource management was prioritized for UNDP support during the 2003-2007 programme cycle through programmes in environmental governance, climate change and biodiversity. The current programme (2008-2012) continued the same priority under outcome 4 of the MCPD: sustainable environmental management.

Improving Capacity to Mainstream Environmental Sustainability: This project focuses on capacity building centred on the Department of Environment and key ministries responsible for the national environmental policies. The project is to improve sharing of information among responsible ministries but also to formalize an environment programme coordination action plan.

The ADR mission did not get any information to gauge the extent to which collaboration has improved among key national policy planning agencies of the Government responsible for environmental policies. The ADR mission found that this project has been very active with the compilation of the greenhouse inventory and integration of climate change into the planning and designing of national infrastructure. The Second Communications project highlighted the need for UNDP to work closely with the Secretariat of the Pacific Regional Environment Programme (SPREP) to improve effectiveness of UNDP initiatives supporting environmental programmes.

The Sustainable Land Management (SLM) project was contributing to raising public awareness, integration of sustainable land management policies into national plans, drafting of Land Act and introducing sustainable farming practices and production techniques. The ADR mission considered the project effective with its outputs leading to modernizing the land use, production and processing methods for cultivation of root crops like yams and animal husbandry linked to a mini abattoir. The project has also led to a review of land-use policy, sustainable leasing conditions and land legislation updates to improve economic use of customary land. The SLM project has contributed to the drafting of Kastom Land Policy, as part of the project's outcome of 'enhancing legal framework for promoting SLM'. The recent mid-term review recommended that completion of Vanuatu's Kastom Land Policy be handed over to the appropriate authority due to significant work involved that may delay project progress. However, feedback to the ADR mission suggested there was still expectation that the project would do more work on the mechanisms for resolution of customary land lease disputes which are critical in ensuring that any disputes are quickly resolved to avoid disruptions to sustainable use of rural customary lands.

Strengthening Community Capacity to Adapt to Environmental Changes and Demands on Natural Resources: The premise of this intervention was that the development of effective community interventions and local actions would inform and guide appropriate upstream policy development, structural changes for stronger institutions and appropriate legislation. UNDP was to assist the Government by working with stakeholders to address concerns and issues of traditional and modern systems, practices and regimes of natural resource management. The ADR mission found that the GEF small grants programme and the sustainable land management projects were considered relatively more visible and effective. This was due to a relatively well-organized national focal point for NGOs, VANGO, and also the adaptation of the forms and procedures by the local GEF focal point to facilitate the participation of the community organizations and NGOs. There was strong positive comments by the CSOs consulted that the GEF small grants project has been adaptable and effective from their perspective. VANGO also indicated that the effectiveness of the project has led to an increase in the number of registered CSOs which usually then seek support from the GEF small grants project. However, it was not possible to gauge whether the capacity of the CSOs to adapt to environmental changes on natural resources has been effectively enhanced.

TUVALU

The CPAP (2008-2012) for Tuvalu identified the following priorities in environment outcome: (a) improving capacity to mainstream environmental sustainability; and (b) strengthening community capacity to adapt to environmental change and demands on natural resources. Environmental sustainability is central to Tuvalu's development, and indeed even to its very survival. Two major projects underway were addressed in this assessment:

- The National Adaptation Plan of Action (NAPA): US$7.8 million ($3.3 million from the GEF) implemented by the Ministry for Natural Resources and the Environment,

- The Sustainable Land Management Project (SLM): US$1.017 million ($0.5 million from the GEF), implemented by the National Environmental Service.

Both projects address common issues and approaches such as land management, coastal erosion, knowledge development, and community participation and awareness. NAPA also focuses on the incorporation of environmental strategies into government policy and budgeting, particularly in public works, agriculture and water management. The SLM focuses on integrating more specifically land resourced and degradation issues into National Development Plans. At the moment, there is no land use plan or policy, although the SLM includes provisions for hiring a consultant to help develop these. In the absence of a plan or policy, the people are free to use their land as they like.

NAPA supports demonstration projects in each island group, five primarily in coastal protection (mangrove and sea walls) and four in water management systems. Some have additional elements such as fish management or adapting agriculture to greater salinity (pulaka pits and breadfruit). More recently, NAPA is considering the Foram sands approach to coastal protection[34] introduced by the Japan International Cooperation Agency. Both projects work with local communities in awareness raising, and participatory planning, and project implementation. The SLM's focus was more on demonstration land use planning activities at the community level. To complicate (or complement) matters more, there was also participation by CSO and, to some extent, overlap with community-level GEF funds. Virtually all sources pointed out that coordination was weak, even though it was essential given the similar nature and overlapping target groups of the projects. Some concerns were raised over lack of coordination not only leading to duplication of efforts, but to detrimental project results. It was noted that NAPA and the SLM came to the same communities with different and sometimes conflicting messages about approaches, or for example, level of remuneration for mangrove tree planting. In addition, the SLM recognized the drawbacks of seawalls, which include trapping seawater and contributing to salination.

The environmental projects are seen as extremely relevant to the country by all respondents given Tuvalu's vulnerable position. There is a recognized level of effectiveness in implementing the projects at the policy/planning level, and also at the community development level where it should be compatible with the local development planning and management process.

Women are very much involved in environmental sustainability, and are, for example, the main mangrove tree planters (which also provides some cash income), although men have land ownership and are the key agricultural producers. The project specifically planned to involve civil society (TANGO) to enhance the role of women and young people in the SLM. A gender analysis was to have been carried out, but in the absence of reports, it is not clear whether this has been done. While some progress has been made in women's participation in community level assemblies, local and traditional councils, as well as Parliament are overwhelmingly male. It was suggested, in a positive way, that any progress in promoting gender equality was due to pressure from donors.

Reducing their **efficiencies**, however, is the lack of coordination mentioned above. In addition, both projects have suffered staff turnovers in a short time, and in the case of NAPA, a nine-month delay caused by personnel issues. In the case of GEF local funds, there were major delays in project approval and funding. In addition, as mentioned above, there is a lack of coordination, with different projects targeting the same population with duplication and at times, conflicting messages.

---

34 Foram is the coral debris sand that washed onto the coral reefs to form Tuvalu in the first place. This project aims to selectively regenerate its formation as coastal protection.

The issue of **sustainability** is similar to other very small Pacific island countries. The human resource base is inadequate to support the range of skills and experience needed to run major government programmes and the many development projects. As in the NAPA project, activities can be delayed by personnel issues around a single position, and inadequate government performance monitoring. Sustainability is sometimes expressed as just being able to keep personnel until the end of the project. A factor contributing to sustainability is the extensive involvement of communities in the planning and implementation of environment projects. According to the SLG evaluation, community-level planning is still very much a 'wish list' approach emphasizing infrastructure projects. Recently, a few projects more socially oriented, and for women and youth, were beginning to appear, which might signal the beginning of a more integral and participatory planning approach. However, capacity, as a key element of sustainability, is still a challenge.

TONGA

Under the 2003-2007 programme cycle, UNDP supported environmental protection and resource management through programmes in environmental governance, climate change and biodiversity, particularly in helping Tonga to meet its obligations in various multilateral environment agreements. The 2008-2012 CPAP supports improved capacity to mainstream environmental sustainability at the national level.

Environmental projects underway with UNDP support include Climate Change Enabling Activity, and Sustainable Land Management. The Climate Change Enabling Activity ($450,000) allows the Government to develop plans to comply with all international obligations. Additional environmental projects are the Persistent Organic Pollutants (POPs) and Ozone-Depleting Substances, and Programme of Work in Protected Areas, implemented by UNEP.

Sustainable Land Management is a four-year programme beginning in 2008, with a total budget of $1,037,493 of which $475,000 is provided by GEF, $335,000 by the Government, and the rest from the SPREP and the Secretariat of the Pacific Community (SPC.) The purpose of the project is to stem land degradation through developing capacity at the individual, institutional and systemic level to manage land use, including mainstreaming into national plans and budgets. The project's focus includes a wide range of issues such as land tenure, pest control, and soil fertility. Sharing techniques and best practices among the countries at the regional level is one of the main advantages of the project. However, limited information regarding results was available to the evaluation team. According to the Ministry of Environment and Climate Change, the project is useful and information/technology sharing in the region is one of its most useful aspects.

SAMOA

Samoa CPAP enlisted a number of projects under outcome of environment and sustainable development'. Notably Samos MCO continues to enjoy a good partnership with non-core funding agencies like GEF and others that continue to provide funding for most of the initiatives in the environment. The main projects in this outcome area are:

- Community-Centred Sustainable Development Project (CCSDP)
- Integrating Climate Change Adaptation into Agriculture and Health (ICCRAH)
- Community-Based Adaptation (CBA)
- Small Grants Programme (SGP)
- Samoa's Capacity Building and Mainstreaming of Sustainable Land Management (SLM)
- Pacific Adaptation to Climate Change (PACC) - Regional
- Pacific Islands Greenhouse Gas Abatement through Renewable Energy Project (PIGGAREP) – Regional

The ADR team was able to interact with a number of the major counterparts and interlocutors. As there was an outcome evaluation which dealt in depth the main criteria of effectiveness, efficiency and sustainability, the ADR interviews focused mostly on strategic aspects of broader effectiveness and UNDP's value added and role in substantive and technical aspects of projects, thereby facilitating achievement of outcomes beyond outputs.

The Government considers that in the area of environment and climate change, the question on effectiveness and stability of programmes are to be considered in light of international intentions and spirit of conventions. The formal institutional arrangements offer the choices of implementation through UNEP, FAO, UNESCO or UNDP. The Government finds UNDP has the expertise and specialty in making that linkage between the conventions and government agencies at the national level, which is considered very useful. The easy access to UNDP locally ensures the flow of interaction and assistance. A senior official indicated that in this region, UNDP is still the leading agency in environment and climate change, unlike many other regions where UNEP is considered as the lead agency. The Government's confidence in the large pool of expertise that UNDP has locally and their technical understanding and appreciation of the local situation creates conditions for effectiveness in implementation. The Ministry of Natural Resources and Environment, however, indicated that in future the Government, for building up its own capacity, would wish to avail funding directly from the open funding windows, which might shrink UNDP's funding access. When that happens, UNDP will still remain the main choice for the Government for accessing other relevant funding sources.

REPUBLIC OF MARSHALL ISLANDS

The two projects in the environment focus area for RMI are:

- **Capacity Building for Sustainable Land Management** (2008-2012; $1,064,000), often referred to as SLM, focuses on land utilization, climate change, capacity building, and planning about how to mainstream land policies that mitigate land degradation as well as build capacity for change in attitude about land use.

- **Action for Development of Marshall Islands Renewable Energies (ADMIRE)** (for 2008-2013; $2,625,000), which aims at increasing the use of renewable energy technologies and by removing barriers for the application of these technologies and the enhancing of institutions' capacity to coordinate, finance, design, supply and maintain and use renewable energy technologies.

Both are complementary, very relevant and needed for RMI given its limited land resources and the increasing cost of fossil fuel. The sustainability of life in an atoll rests on how people manage their scarce resources of land and how renewable energy sources like the wind, sun or tide, which are abundant, are put to use. By the same yardstick, these two projects, which address as their objectives the major problems of land management, access to clean and affordable energy and climate change mitigation, would undoubtedly be considered most relevant and timely.

Unfortunately, both projects are delayed by almost two years and one of them, the SLM, has achieved very little substantive activities. Its inception workshop was done by an outside consultant only in January 2011 three years after it began. There has been little effective leadership coupled with the resignation of senior staff. As for the ADMIRE project, some progress was reported during the third year of implementation, including its contribution to the passing of RMI's Renewable Energy and Energy Efficiency Bill, review of RMI's building codes in line with the national energy policy and climate change policy framework, awareness events and discussions on institutionalizing of renewable energy in RMI's national training vocational programmes. Both projects involve the partnership of RMI, GEF and UNDP plus minor co-funding groups. UNDP has expanded its standard monitoring practices from quarterly checks to extraordinary (detailed staff assignment) measures that involve undertaking project activities. A turnaround in implementation is reported through the detailed assignment arrangements. e.g., the ADMIRE project collaborated with SPC/EU North REP project on awareness activities and energy demand surveys in outer island communities. Additionally, the ADMIRE project secured a site for installation of wind-monitoring system and commenced preparation for mid-term review. The SLM project commenced the development of a database that would ensure efficient monitoring of coastal development to be institutionalized by the Environment Protection Authority (EPA). Additional support through extraordinary arrangements needs to be maintained in order for RMI to reap the benefits of such projects.

PALAU

Environment and sustainable management is one of the main areas of intervention under the current CPAP (2008-2012).

The project on Sustainable Economic Development through Renewal Energy Applications (SEDREA) will widen the scope of the EU-funded solar energy development project by addressing all potential renewable energy resources in Palau in meeting the energy demands of the Palauan economy. It will address the GEF climate change strategic priorities, and would involve activities that would overcome/remove barriers to the development and widespread use of RE technologies (RETs), as well as addressing an increased access to financing of RE projects, establishment and implementation of regulatory frameworks that are supportive of RE, and productive uses of RE in line with enhancing socio-economic growth in the country's rural areas.

Since its inception in 2009, the SEDREA project is progressing quite well. It is now enabling the wide use of solar power on and off-grid systems supported by the National Development Bank of Palau (NDBP) with provision for loans which is reducing the energy consumption and power bills for families who have taken such loan. The project made it possible for ordinary Palauan families to access loans with terms of either 10 or 20 years and purchase a solar unit (of 3.4 kwp, with 2kits of 1.7 kwp) and thereby enjoy a substantially reduced power bill of about US$100 a month, depending on the efficiency of their unit and their level of power consumption. The NDBP had ploughed a million US dollars into a renewable energy fund window with a clearly defined and organized fund mobilization and financing scheme. There is now the move to draw up a MOU which provides for the Palau Public Utilities Corporation to purchase electricity through this system from consumers which would enable ordinary consumers to benefit fully from this project. As the system improves from greater efficiency, the benefits are likely to increase as the loan system becomes streamlined, and available technological options increased. Meanwhile, the percentage of subsidies is reduced on annual basis with subsidy completely dropping off in 2016. The SEDREA project is more than just subsidized loans. Its partnership with the private sector for supplying systems, installation and maintenance, which is critical for this new market of renewable energy applications (PV system), is of great significance in the future sustainability of work undertaken.

In two other projects – Sustainable Land Management (SLM) and National Capacity Self Assessment for Global Environment Management (NCSA) – there is a real attempt in the projects to address the needs of Palau. In the former, for example, the evaluator witnessed firsthand in Airai project area workers were trying to plan their new town to ensure they maintained acceptable land-use practices in construction of houses. They also had to adhere to a master plan which was also developed by their own representatives in their state. This was a good example of how new settlements near major towns can be environmentally managed by following some requirements relating land use issues and other building requirements set by the municipal or rural authorities.

Under the project, there was also work on taro experimental farms near a mangrove area as part of PACC. The attempt in this project is to breed new varieties of taro using ones from Fiji and

Samoa together with local varieties, to produce a salt water resistant taro. The taro in the pilot field was growing well, different varieties were showing different growth patterns, and characteristics and the results would only be known after the harvesting of the plants. If successful, this could be a ground-breaking exercise.

In the NCSA project, the aim was to examine local capacity in Palau to meet needs and obligations under three conventions signed namely, the UN Convention on Biological Diversity (UNCBD), the UN Convention on Climate Change (UNFCCC), and the UN Convention to Combat Desertification (UNCCD). These important conventions, ratified by Palau in the second half of 1999, were adopted by the UN in the early 1990s. The Palau Government wanted to make sure it was discharging the obligations it had committed itself to. Palau's NCSA produced an action plan and resource mobilization strategy which highlighted the need for strengthening capacity at all levels: systemic – through establishment and enforcement of policies, legislations, coherent national framework of government policy and regulations for integrated environmental management; institutional – through establishment of government agency to coordinate implementation of activities under all three Rio Conventions and other environmental initiatives; and individual – through training and upskilling of staff capacities to effectively implement activities under all three Rio Conventions. There is clear evidence from professional observers and assessors of real commitment on the part of the Government that this project was to be undertaken and findings implemented.

In fact, in all three projects, the contribution of the Government of Palau was significant. In two of the three projects, the Government was the biggest contributor, even bigger than the GEF. In the SEDREA project, for example, which has attracted a lot of attention in Palau at the moment, of a total project funding of US$4,400,000, the Palau Government contributed in cash, $3,425,000, which is close to 80 percent of the total funding. GEF contribution in this project was $975,000. This demonstrates the level of commitment of the Government of Palau and also reflects the level of consciousness on the importance of the issues of access to clean and sustainable energy and sustainable environmental management in Palau. One of the strongest features of the projects studied in Palau was the feeling of ownership of projects by the people. It should be noted that while this is one of the factors responsible for the success of the SEDREA project, the other one was the commitment of the Palau Energy Office, support from the NDBP, the PPU and the technical support and monitoring of the UNDP MCO, Suva and the national JP office in Palau.

KIRIBATI

Improving Capacity to Mainstream Environmental Sustainability Policies into the National Planning Systems of Government: The ADR mission found that this project on improving capacity of the Ministry of Environment, Lands and Agriculture to mainstream environmental sustainability for the 2008-2011 period has been refocused on strengthening of the planning capabilities of the Ministry of Finance and Economic with the proposed setting up of a database on environmental and sustainable management information. Information from this database will feed into the monitoring and evaluation of environmental programmes in development.

The project on Second National Communications has enabled Kiribati as a signatory of the UNFCC to prepare a national communication comprising a national greenhouse gas inventory, abatement analysis; and vulnerability and adaptation assessments. The ADR mission noted that a consultant has been recruited to assist with the preparation of the three national communication components. The National Adaptation Programme of Action (NAPA) project details the long-term framework of adaptation for Kiribati. The ADR mission found that this project has been completed with the achievement of its project outputs.

The initiative to strengthen community capacity to adapt to environmental changes and demands on natural resources included project activities for mangrove management, sustainable land management at the community level and GEF community small grants projects under the auspices of the Ministry of Environment, Lands and Agriculture in partnership with the Kiribati Association of Non-Government Organizations (KANGO). The initiatives supporting the Kiribati communities to effectively manage and sustainably use their environment as well as natural and cultural resources have included effective delivery of community mangrove management, sustainable land management policies and legislation. The GEF small grant projects administered through KANGO and subcontracted to Ecocare has covered 10 community projects and has worked well until it started encountering some delays. The ADR mission found that the project outputs for the GEF small grants projects have been delayed due to some institutional issues involving the capacity of KANGO to effectively discharge of its responsibilities as an implementing agency.

FIJI

The MCDP outcome of environment and sustainable management has three projects in Fiji:

- National capacity self assessment for global environmental management
- Fiji sustainable land management project
- Developing capacity to monitor, evaluate and communicate climate change

National Capacity Self-Assessment in environment started in 2008. As a signatory to three multilateral environmental agreements, it was really timely and relevant to Fiji. It helped in identifying gaps and constraints at three levels: systemic, institutional and individual. The project had a fresh assessment of the environmental legislation that was passed in 2005. It identified certain gaps and inadequacies which was very helpful. It also had a strong capacity development component. This output of the project has national implications and its impact will cut across many sectors and the whole country. The assessment also addresses an institutional reform issue that is an important output, which will provide direct input for some reforms in the near future.

In Fiji UNDP's work in the energy sector has moved from enabling activities (i.e., soft-type intervention) to implementation support of hardware configurations and installations. The energy projects are fine examples of this shift in approach that has resulted in Fiji Government's shift of priorities to promoting renewable energy. Fiji is the first country in the Pacific to establish tax-free incentives on renewable energy technology. Fiji has also recently expanded its bio-fuel industry by establishing bio-fuel mills in outer islands, which UNDP contributed to from its TRAC-funded bio-fuel project.

The Government considers that urban areas have more pressing demands on many environmental issues because of drifting and concentration of population. The demand in rural areas, on the other hand, is more in the area of conservation of biodiversity and ecosystems. But the Government has ensured the presence of an environment official in each of the 14 provinces. There is a general national awareness for conservation of biodiversity. As concentration in urban areas breeds more environmental issues, the Government works closely with local government. While addressing pressing urban issues, the ministry still has an eye on local needs. The new direction is to cover peri-urban and rural areas for which additional budget is being secured.

FEDERATED STATES OF MICRONESIA

During the current programme period, the main UNDP environmental initiative in FSM is the Sustainable Land Management project, with a total budget of $1.4 million comprising a GEF contribution of $500,000, a government co-funding component of $933,300 the largest portion of which came from the four states of FSM (totaling $440,639). The implementation was being carried out in the four states of FSM, which involved NGOs, community groups and the four state governments. It involved various practices and approaches of sustainable land management. Although it created great interest, it demanded a lot more flexibility in management procedures and especially in financial responsiveness and accountability.

A mid-term evaluation of the project conducted in June 2011 by an independent evaluator in accordance with GEF requirements was very supportive and enthusiastic about the progress made. It strongly recommended greater flexibility in adjusting budgets to expedite implementation of the project. The mid-term evaluation highlighted that it considered the project 'highly replicable' and noted the 'excellent collaboration and co-financing with other ongoing related programs in FSM' including other 'practices of recycling programmes, community gardening and composting, tree replacing and other actions that achieved immediate results'.

In the assessment of the mission, this was a highly relevant and effective project and the interest it had generated through its collaboration with both state government and their NGO partners was noteworthy. The sense of ownership it generated through involvement of both government (central and state levels) and non-government organizations, in addition to wide community participation made it potentially sustainable. The distinctive feature of this project is that its implementation is in the hands of the four states and the major role of the national office is with funding. The mid-term review of the project shared the same view and urged greater flexibility of UNDP in both financial and administrative procedures. In a focus group discussion, attention was drawn to the 'sluggish' pace of implementation, which requires more intensive monitoring, by UNDP and a greater degree of application of decision-making at the project level.

The SLM project is an important one for FSM. As pointed out by its MTE evaluator, the project is drawing a lot of traction and is obviously seen to be relevant to the country's major challenges over environmental degradation. Many issues were raised in focus group discussions about the need for UNDP to be more responsive to some of the problems raised about its procedures, both administrative and financial. These points have implications on the positioning of UNDP: its flexibility, its devolution of authority and its relationships with other regional Pacific organization like the SPC, for example, and its capability in managing its downstream activities.

NIUE

During the current programme cycle (2008-2012), the environment portfolio includes an early recovery programme, Sustainable Land Management, PACC, Pacific Island Greenhouse Gas Abatement through Renewable Energy (PIGGAREP) and CCSDP.

The PACC project in Niue is a four-year initiative ($750,000 from UNDP/GEF, $50,000 from the Government, $497,000 from AusAID) addressing water issues. Niue's water supply is subterranean. There is underground water lens but the high cost of required infrastructure, operational costs for pumping the water to homes make its use prohibitive as a regular source. The only other affordable source of water is rain, and it must be managed carefully. Local catchment and storage will reduce vulnerability to climate change, including storms or blackouts that could interrupt the current distribution system. Among the achievements are the completed policy changes based on wide consultation; a socio-economic study underway, a procurement bid process underway for community/household level water catchment systems/tanks; and GIS-based data gathering for better analysis. The planned vulnerability assessment has not taken place, mainly because funds have not arrived. The environmental programme is highly relevant given Niue's vulnerability. Water and soil depletion are major threats to Niue's sustainability. Rain is irregular already, and this year, for example, mango trees are not bearing fruit because of off-season rain.

The CCSPD also seemed to be the vehicle for coordination among projects. While the PACC project, for example, had no relation to any other project or service besides the integrated water resource management unit, members of the CCSDPs seemed to be aware of and participating in several projects including the SLM, renewable energy projects, PACC water infrastructure and overall village development approaches. In an example of the local-level coordination, the head of the organic farmers is a member of the local CCSDP, involved in PACC water activities, involved in soil fertility management and working on solar power initiatives. This degree of coordination is less apparent at the national level.

COOK ISLANDS

Environmental Sustainability. The National Environment Service is the national focal point for all environmental projects of GEF and the UNDP. Like most Pacific islands, Cook Islands are vulnerable to natural disasters and the long-term threat of climate change. Particularly vulnerable are the communication infrastructure (harbours and airports), the tourism industry, and the low-lying atolls.

Projects undertaken by Cook Islands or still underway include:

- CKI Second National Communication (SNC)
- Persistent Organic Pollutants (POP)
- Pacific Island Greenhouse Gas Abatement through Renewable Energy (PIGGAREP)
- Regional Sustainable Land Management (SLM)
- Pacific Adaptation to Climate Change (PACC) – regional
- Community Centred Sustainable Development Project (CCSDP)

One of the largest of these is the PACC project, implemented by the Ministry of Infrastructure and Planning, with an initial budget of US$800,000, and US$500,000 from Australia through PACC+. Implementation set to begin in 2008 was delayed until 2009, with a completion date of 2014. According to project management, the participation in PACC was greatly facilitated by the two-year enabling project (2005-2007).

Cook Islands participate as one of 13 countries in the region in the PACC project. This is the first project in the region drawing on the Special Climate Change Fund (SCCF), managed by GEF. It participates along with three other countries in a coastal management programme. The original plan was to complement the government plan to redevelop the Manihiki airport in the Northern Island group (with New Zealand funds) with a coastal vulnerability assessment, developing guidelines to integrate coastal climate risk management into relevant plans using participatory methodology; and training key technical staff. However, with the delay in plans, New Zealand funding expired, and Cook Islands switched to a similar plan in Mangaia, for a harbour. The harbour has been rebuilt with national funds.

The PACC framework includes three elements: mainstreaming climate adaptation plans into national development plans to ensure sustainability, which has not yet been done in CKI; involving communities in vulnerability assessments and subsequent planning (the Island Council and local groups are involved); and technical support in assessing risk management. In the CKI case, a geospatial analysis of the harbour and surrounding area in Mangaia is being undertaken with technical assistance from SOPAC. According to the Ministry of Infrastructure and Planning, the specialized expertise to do this, and more importantly, the expensive equipment, is not available in CKI.

NAURU

Mainstreaming environment and energy, and adapting to climate change has been identified as a priority area for UNDP intervention during the current programme period.

The Second Communications project will assist Nauru fulfil its obligations under the UNFCCC. The project is expected to help Nauru prepare its Second National Communication (SNC) comprising three major elements: a national greenhouse gas inventory (GHGI), abatement analysis, and vulnerability and adaptation assessments. The SNC report would highlight Nauru's status in terms of its GHG contribution, which sectors and geographical locations are most vulnerable to climate change and map out strategies to mitigate and adapt to climate change. The ADR mission noted that a consultant has been recruited to assist with the preparation of the three national communication components. Based on analysis of secondary data sources, the mission concluded that the tools produced through the SNC project are generally informing policy-level/decisions regarding mitigation and adaptation. Being a non-LDC with limited access to climate finance, Nauru considers the SNC project critical in assisting to produce its Adaptation Framework as well as support to institutionalize climate change through the recently established CC Unit.

The Sustainable Land Management (SLM) project is designed to fully integrate into the national plans and policies sustainable land management best practices that will fully address land degradation issues. The goal of Nauru's SLM is to contribute to maintaining and improving ecosystem stability, integrity, functions and services while enhancing sustainable livelihoods. This will be done by building Nauru's capacity to implement a comprehensive regime for sustainable land management and to ensure that the SLM is mainstreamed into all levels of decision-making. By the end of the project, land degradation issues should be fully recognized in national development plans and sector action plans, such as those for urban development, transport, agriculture and biodiversity. The SLM should also be integrated into relevant policy, laws and educational/training programmes, using integrated land-use planning to underpin such initiatives.

The ADR mission noted that a number of public awareness campaigns had been undertaken and the capacity of the Department of Commerce, Industry and Environment had been supported with training in global information systems. However, the country has to go some way to achieve the intended outcomes of the project.

The GEF Small Grants Programme administered by UNDP and implemented by Nauru Island Association of NGOs (NIANGO) targets community development initiatives promoting environmental protection, poverty elimination and sustainable livelihoods. The programme had come to a standstill with ongoing dispute between NIANGO and the Ministry of Finance on the release of funding for the community projects and payments to NIANGO. The situation has compounded with the leaders of the 11 communities lodging their protest against NIANGO governance arrangements.

GEF small grants project started with two community projects approved in the first year. A further three community projects were approved in the second and third year. The NIANGO coordinator implementing the projects demonstrated that she had good communication skills and good understanding of the basic project and financial management knowledge to guide the communities in processing their projects and guiding them in their financial accounting and reporting. However, the gap in reporting and communications with the community project stakeholders appeared to have adversely affected the effectiveness of the community projects, which were further aggravated when the disbursements of the funds were frozen by the Ministry of Finance.

Chapter 5
STRATEGIC POSITIONING

5.1 STRATEGIC RELEVANCE AND RESPONSIVENESS

The Fiji and Samoa Multi-Country Programme Documents (MCPD) for the periods 2003-2007 and 2008-2012 addressed a subregional development agenda relevant to all 14 countries and presented an overarching strategic programme focus as a basis for individual country projects and initiatives. The alignment of UNDP-funded programmes and projects with the needs and priorities of the governments was ensured through close and iterative consultations with the governments of the Pacific island countries. The governments across the Pacific appreciated this consultative nature of programme development. The MCPDs bear a close alignment with country priorities as reflected in national development plans, the MDGs, the regional UNDAF 2008-2012 and the Pacific Plan for regional integration and cooperation.

5.1.1 RELEVANCE AND RESPONSIVENESS

The most distinctive characteristic of UNDP strategy in the region is its sustained partnership in the areas which squarely represent priority development issues of the PICs and UNDP's areas of competence. UNDP has maintained its longer term focus and support in the areas of poverty, governance, crisis prevention and recovery and environment. These areas represent critically important issues with evolving depth and complexity, requiring advocacy and adequate evidence for generating policy support and strategic directions. The longer term support assists the countries in sustainability of the initiatives by allowing the space and time for the country to develop a national position on the issue, internalizing it in the institutional structure and developing adequate capacity to carry on the function.

The strategic relevance and responsiveness of UNDP is the result of continuous consultation with the PICs on national and subregional issues, detailed consultative mechanism for developing CPAPs and projects. UNDP's responsiveness to adjust with changing needs and circumstances is widely appreciated. The continuity in the programme focus supported by strategic thinking over the last two programme cycles have created the space for the national side to have sustainability elements organized for UNDP-supported projects. It also provided a good basis for a stable programmatic dialogue.

UNDP's best responsiveness has been demonstrated in times of natural disasters. This was evident during the recent natural disasters in Fiji, Samoa, Tonga, Solomon Islands and Cook Island. The governments widely appreciated the ability of UNDP to move promptly and mobilize the possible inputs for a disaster assessment followed by relief. The evaluation team received excellent feedback from the direct counterparts at the field level on the quality of work and their effectiveness. UNDP has also been responsive to changes in governance environments in countries of the region. UNDP's response to unwarranted political changes in countries was always guided by the tolerance, understanding and protecting the wider interest of the people.

5.1.2 EFFECTIVENESS AND EFFICIENCY

However, overall effectiveness and efficiency in all four outcome areas show mixed tendencies. Project formulations many times reflect lack of technical and incisive analysis of the real issues to be addressed, project designs and approaches reflect adoption of limited options, lack of gender analysis, and inadequate assessment of counterpart institutional capacities. Process delays of approval, procurement, and fund transfer are generally the norm across the board. The most important gap was apparent in monitoring provision of technical oversight to quality assure policy-oriented outputs. Project monitoring reports, project progress reports, notes from project visits and meetings were frequently lacking and, when available, did not contain required depth of information. The number of projects running time delays in implementation is substantial. The dynamics of maintaining multifaceted coordination in the pace of delivering outputs, generating the necessary institutional preparedness within the counterpart agencies led, in many cases, to little visible progress towards outcome. These issues were repeated in almost all countries at the government counterpart levels, by the participating CSOs and the donors. They can be easily addressed through stronger management oversight and vigilant monitoring systems.

5.2 COMPARATIVE STRENGTH

In all the countries visited, the governments reaffirmed to the mission their trust and confidence in UNDP as a neutral development partner and broker in sensitive issues of conflict reconciliation and political governance. UNDP has judiciously applied this advantage whenever there was a need for its services. UNDP support to Solomon Islands during the period of conflict and later support in the Truth and Reconciliation Commission, in supporting demobilization of rebels were mentioned as examples of such services. Recent support in moving the Convention on Corruption within some countries (Vanuatu, Tuvalu) was also recognized.

UNDP is recognized for its expertise and niche in governance, policy-oriented poverty work, crisis prevention and recovery, and environmental governance. In these areas, UNDP is well known globally and is able to draw from the intellectual capital it has developed over many decades of work all over the developing world. The expertise has been developed out of practical work in various development situations and a cadre of professional specialized on those areas also within the organization. This stock of applied intellectual strength and the ability to draw on that strength places UNDP in a unique valued position. The manifestation of this dimension is seen in the combined and complementary work of the MCOs and the Pacific Centre which has demonstrated technical proficiency in the areas of MDGs, poverty, governance, gender, conflict and security, disaster prevention, and financial inclusion. The mission heard many commendations from the countries on their high-quality work and timely response.

UNDP is considered a repository of global experiences and knowledge in development considering its global outreach and network of presence. It is also considered a gateway for linkage and accessing services from the wider UN system specialized agencies which are not represented in the Pacific. The ability to reach out to such an extensive network for development solutions is indeed considered valuable by the Pacific countries. This also differentiates UNDP from the other regional organizations in that their experience draws from only regional sources.

Again, the various publications on regional and thematic issues by the Pacific Centre have been recognized by development professionals, many government officials, and regional organizations as a UNDP contribution to stock of knowledge on Pacific. However, it was also mentioned that this knowledge broker role should be more visible at the project-level work.

5.3 PARTNERSHIP

UNDP has been a stable and useful development partners for the PICs for many decades. Its involvement has spanned many areas of development, with a variety of roles: as an initiator, facilitator, provocateur, catalyser, and implementer. In that regard, UNDP lent a helping hand to many spheres of development. Feedback from a wide range of stakeholders has indicated that UNDP standing in the Pacific is disproportionately high in relation to the resources it directly contributes. Even those with specific criticisms of UNDP's role generally have a favourable view of its contribution to the subregion. UNDP achieved this recognition primarily by forging strategic partnerships with various actors and stakeholders, and dealing with partners in a way that generates trust and mutual respect. UNDP has systematically pursued and developed its partnerships with Pacific island governments, multilateral and bilateral donor agencies, the regional organizations and Council of Regional Organizations of the Pacific (CROP) agencies, and CSOs and NGOs to support its development effectiveness.

5.3.1 GOVERNMENTS

Partnership with government agencies is usually at the level of designated counterpart coordinating ministries (usually planning or finance) and principal line ministries that are main counterparts of the projects. Over the years, this relationship with coordinating agencies has transformed into a friendly relationship of shared values, trust and respect. UNDP's political neutrality, respect for national sovereignty, appreciation of development constraints and transparent position have helped it earn this special position of confidence among the PICs. The mission saw this recognition across the board. In spite of the physical distance from the MCOs and the fact that communication to a large extent is virtual with most PICs interspersed with periodic visits by UNDP management and professionals, the evaluation mission felt that there is a certain level of understanding of the constraints and gaps that emanate as a result. One observation is that the image of UNDP is still confined to the central level and the organization does not enjoy much familiarity at the subnational or local levels. This is understandable and can be expanded with more project work at decentralized and outer island level.

UNDP's close access to central coordinating agencies is seen as an asset by the UN system agencies, which usually operate through their line sectoral ministries. Although this strong relationship has proven to be useful for programmatic purposes and considered effective, the few areas where the evidence of UNDP footprint is visible in influencing major development policy or reform at the macro level are: mainstreaming MDGs into national policies, raising the profile of anti-poverty measures, and the support to ratification of global conventions. The potential areas of outcome are empowering national parliaments, local governance, and aid-effectiveness mechanisms. In the case of micro states (viz., Tokelau, Niue, and Nauru), UNDP's partnership efforts seemed to have lesser depth due to relatively small magnitude of programme activities and lack of availability of usual institutional structure and capacity in governments. The strategy of programme and modality of interventions in micro states require a different strategy from bigger island states, such as pursuing joint programmes with partners and having more integrated project structure (with multiple streams) with single project management to alleviate administrative burden on the governments.

5.3.2 CIVIL SOCIETY AND NGOS

The evaluation team had some good interaction with civil society organizations in many of the PICs. At the national level and advocacy work, UNDP has been able to create a reasonable engagement with NGOs and CSOs. The extent and depth of the relationships were based on the availability, organization and preparedness of the CSOs and NGOs. Many of the PIC governments were very favourably disposed towards the role of CSOs in development. But important utilization of CSO/NGOs has been at project level implementation. In smaller atoll countries, there have been significant CSO roles in GEF SGP projects, decentralization and local governance projects, CCSDP, coastal and marine resource management, environment and climate change issues. These partnerships have been generally very effective and results oriented, although in a few cases there were issues of efficiency and lack of competence. The positive experience of working with CSOs should be upscaled in other areas and should be a preferred modality for all downstream community outreach work. The CSOs and NGOs interviewed held UNDP in high esteem but at the apex level many of them felt they were not being leveraged enough in bigger national initiatives.

5.3.3 UN SYSTEM

UNDP's partnership is very strong with the UN system agencies in the Pacific. This is further facilitated by the organization's Resident Coordinator function. In the Pacific, this partnership and coordination is extremely important because of the dispersed locations of the countries. The coordination is also important to minimize the aid-related transaction overload on the PICs that have limited human resource capacity. During the current cycle, the UN system operated under one UNDAF for all 14 countries which provides a converging framework for development assistance. The presence of multiple UN agencies in Fiji (12) makes the coordination work more complex and time consuming. While commending UNDP on the positive partnership and the RC for excellent coordination work, the UN agencies also pointed out a few anomalies such as the fact that UNDP has two RCs in the Pacific while all other stations have only one.

The evaluation team assessed that the UN coordination was working very well with clear leadership. There is a current initiative under the RC to move to a new level of collaboration among the UN agencies in developing joint programmes. The recent opening of UN Joint Presence Offices in all countries of Fiji MCO except Tonga (which is under discussion) is another positive step in coordination. This step has been widely applauded and raised the expectation of the countries for better coordination with UNDP and other agencies. While the level of UNDP partnership with UN system is considered excellent, it requires demonstrating some concrete value-added products and services in support of development. Hopefully that will be a point of deliberation for the upcoming UNDAF exercise.

5.3.4 DONORS

UNDP has progressively forged partnerships with a wide range of development partners. A major portion of the funds for UNDP programme comes from bilateral donors or other multilateral sources notably GEF. Australia, New Zealand and the European Union are the principal donor partners for the Pacific. Each UNDP programme cluster involves other development partners in funding or implementation. Every donor has its own reason for utilizing UNDP as a channel for funding. Because of its resource mobilization necessity, UNDP has to develop a long-term relationship with each potential donor, based on mutual confidence and common appreciation of UNDP's relative advantages and strengths.

Discussion with donor partners suggests that these partnerships so far worked well. The donors consider the governments' confidence in UNDP, its ability to get into sensitive areas and territories as well as its accountability and network of partners as its comparative strength. UNDP's elaborate development administration apparatus and systems of delivery across the Pacific which emerged and matured over many years of practice and refinements draws specific confidence of donors to remain as partners. They are also aware of UNDP's weaknesses in terms of slow delivery, complex procurement and financial rules, slow adaptability to emerging situations. Overall, from the interviews with the donors, the evaluation team concluded that UNDP has managed the relationship with donors reasonably well. However, UNDP needs to take a dynamic and global view of future funding windows like GEF, where there are indications of dwindling resources and change of policies that might affect UNDP's uninterrupted resource flow in environmental programmes.

5.3.5 REGIONAL ORGANIZATIONS

The Pacific has a network of regional organizations and institutions (11) which play an important role in addressing shared development challenges. Due to the scattered layout of the PICs over a vast region, their smallness of size and limited population and resources, regional cooperation was considered as having the potential to address many of the constraints to development in the Pacific. The regional organizations offer numerous development benefits to its members by:

- introducing economies of scale, allowing small countries to benefit from services that they may not otherwise be able to afford or access,
- sharing the costs of (and human resources for) providing specialized public goods,
- strengthening Pacific regional cohesion by jointly addressing common development challenges, and speaking with a common voice beyond the region,
- providing a catalyst for change in the respective countries, and
- supplementing local capacity.

From time to time, these regional organizations at the highest level set many development goals and standards which the PICs are normally committed to. The most recent and overarching is the Pacific Plan which was signed at the 2005 Pacific Islands Forum Leaders' Meeting in order to create stronger and deeper links among the countries of the region. The Pacific Plan seeks out regional approaches and practical steps to enhance and stimulate economic growth, sustainable development, good governance; and security.

UNDP has a long history of cooperation and partnership with the regional organizations notably the PIFS, SPC/SOPAC, FFA/SPREP. The current UNDAF is fully aligned with the Pacific Plan and this alignment and consistency is reaffirmed in most programme documents. UNDP is currently actively involved in many other regional engagements: implementation of the Cairns Compact on development coordination, and facilitation of DPCC (regional roundtable of Development Partners on Climate Change).

UNDP's relationship with the regional architecture has been pursued through both the MCOs and the Pacific Centre's regional programming. Both the UNDAF and the current regional programme of UNDP implemented by the Pacific Centre are fully aligned with the Pacific Plan. Some illustrations of initiatives pursued by the MCOs in support of partnership with the regional organizations are:

- the SPREP on climate change and biodiversity programmes (led by Samoa MCO, supported by Fiji MCO in their countries, with technical backstopping from APRC, Bangkok);
- the SPC on integrated water management (led by Fiji MCO, supported by Samoa MCO in their countries, with technical backstopping from APRC Bangkok);
- the SPC on renewable energy (led by Samoa MCO, supported by Fiji MCO in their countries, with technical backstopping from APRC, Bangkok);
- the FFA on oceanic fisheries management (led by Fiji MCO, supported by Samoa MCO in their countries, with technical backstopping from APRC Bangkok);
- the PIFS on development effectiveness (co-led by Fiji MCO and PC);
- the PIFS and the USP on the Pacific Solution Exchange (co-led by Fiji MCO and PC);
- the PIFS and the SPREP on climate finance and development coordination in the area of climate change (led by Fiji MCO through DPCC) and many others.
- UNDP (Fiji and Samoa MCOs and APRC) have been involved in energy working groups and related regional meetings.

Many of the Pacific Centre's activities over the years have been developed to respond to priorities identified in the Pacific Plan and have involved one or more of the CROP agencies and/or regional NGO umbrella organization in the implementation.

For example, for the Pacific Centre CPR team, this has led to positioning of a UNDP-funded adviser in the PIFS to carry out a jointly agreed work plan on security issues; work with the SPC/SOPAC on disaster risk management, which is governed by an exchange of letters. In the case of the Pacific Financial Inclusion Programme (PFIP), the PIFS is represented on the investment committee and PFIP progress is reported on at the annual Forum Economic Ministers Meeting. For governance, there have been a range of joint activities with the PIFS, including coordinated work on UNCAC, Freedom of Information the regional ombudsman initiative and women and leadership. For the poverty and MDGs team, there is joint work with the PIFS, the SPC and the USP on MDG tracking and national planning, as well as private-sector development. Besides there are close programme-based links with the FFA and the SPREP.

Over the years, many of the regional organizations have developed and implemented regional and country-based programmes in similar areas as UNDP. Accordingly, there are signs of emerging overlap and a sense of crowding each other out in some areas of operation. The PIFS recognized the value of UNDP's additionality in the security sector and financial inclusion programme. The SPC/SOPAC indicated that their potential and capacity is under-utilized by UNDP and there are certainly potential for more engagement. However, there were records of some excellent missed opportunities to work in partnership which failed due to weak commitment by the SPC such as regional framework of support drafted by UNDP with the Sustainable Land Management working group for the region (including the SPC and the SPREP).

The PICs have a sense of ownership of the regional organizations, and it will be wise to develop a mutually beneficial partnership equation with them. The strategic issues UNDP will have to address in the near future is where does UNDP provide value added to the regional policy disccourse? What are the distinct comparative advantages of UNDP vs. CROP agencies, considering that the latter operate not only at the regional but also at the country level? The implications of the questions could be far reaching for UNDP. It might profile UNDP's options to remain as a provider of technical assistance or moving up the value chain to become a broker for global cutting-edge knowledge and solutions, while CROP agencies would become development assistance providers of first resort vis-a-vis the countries.

This requires a more thorough perspective and analysis, possibly through a focused review and a strategy to mange it before it becomes too much of a challenge. The evaluation team did not have adequate time and preparedness to probe deeper into the questions and prospect some feasible options, as the focus of the ADR is on national development results.

5.4 CONTRIBUTION TO UN VALUES AND CROSS-CUTTING ISSUES

5.4.1 HUMAN RIGHTS

As part of the UN system, UNDP carries a special responsibility to comply with and use the internationally agreed-upon norms and standards as normative principles of its work. It also includes the obligation of assisting the countries to ratify and implement the standards agreed to in various UN forums. Among these UNDP is committed to promote realization of human rights, championing and supporting the MDGs and the principle of gender equality.

While UNDAF outcome 2.3 states that "Pacific Island countries are aware and protect human rights and make available mechanisms to claim them", there was no specific country programming in support of human rights in any of the MCPDs. Also, there was no priority accorded to HRBA programming approaches. However, the Pacific Centre has a dedicated human rights advisor, who has worked closely with OHCHR, UNWOMEN and RRRT to promote human rights. The Centre provided training and mentoring support to NGOs to participate in the Commission on the Status of Women in 2008 and 2009. The Centre has also produced a number of HR-related publications in terms of law reform and human rights:

- In partnership with UNIFEM Pacific, the Pacific Centre has published 'Translating CEDAW Into Law: CEDAW Legislative Compliance in Nine Pacific Island Countries', which contains both 113 concrete indicators to measure legislative compliance with CEDAW but also completed national compliance reviews for FS Micronesia, Fiji, Kiribati, Marshall Islands, Papua New Guinea, Samoa, Solomon Islands, Tuvalu and Vanuatu. The Pacific Centre subsequently completed and published 'Translating CEDAW Into Law, CEDAW Legislative Compliance in the Cook Islands'. Support continues to the Cook Islands Government to develop and begin implementing its law reform programme to advance its implementation of CEDAW.

- The Pacific Centre in partnership with UNAIDS RRRT/SPC has published 'Enabling Effective Responses to HIV in Pacific Island Countries: Options for Human Rights-Based Legislative Reform', as well as national human rights compliance reviews of all laws relevant to HIV issues for each of the 15 PICs it serves.

5.4.2 GENDER EQUALITY

According to the Pacific UNDAF, "addressing gender inequality is fundamental to development and integrally linked to a rights-based approach. Gender inequality is manifest in unequal access to resources and property, high incidence of sexual and domestic violence, and under-representation of women in decision-making in public life and local and national politics. National women's machinery in government is generally low in the hierarchy of government structures, poorly resourced". In addition, national policies are not harmonized with international commitments and two countries have not yet ratified CEDAW.

The mid-term evaluation of the UNDAF noted that only one of the 10-12 outcomes for each country and the region as a whole explicitly mentioned gender. Others used words like 'equitable', 'inclusive', or human rights. Little attention had been paid to gender at the national plan levels. Gender analysis was generally uneven and there were few linkages between UNDAF and national plans of action for women and few references to key documents such as the Beijing Plan of Action or CEDAW. In the few examples studied, there were no programme links with national women's offices, which tended to be underfunded, understaffed and mixed with somewhat surprising other government responsibilities that were the main focus of the ministries.

The ADR found a number of good gender-specific, or women's empowerment projects operating at the regional level. For example, connected with the programme to support Parliament is a very high-profile effort to promote temporary special measures to increase women's representation in Parliament, and in some cases excellent empowerment and advocacy through mock Women's Parliaments. Other governance issues include the analysis of national legislation for compliance to CEDAW ('Translating CEDAW into Law: CEDAW Legislative Compliance in Nine Pacific Island Countries'). In the case of Cook Islands, this was carried a step forward into technical advice in drafting new CEDAW-compliant family law legislation for Parliamentary approval. These initiatives were accomplished with the technical and financial resources of the UNDP Pacific Centre. The Pacific Centre has also been responsible for other important initiatives for empowering women, including ensuring high level of participation of women in the Pacific financial inclusion programme which sets and enforces targets, support to the establishment of a regional working group on women, peace and security, among others.

At the MCO and national levels, progress on gender has been slow and varied across countries and projects depending more on the capacity and outlook of the individuals involved than on a common UNDP understanding. Gender is interpreted quite differently across the staff and partners and given different weight in programme planning. To some extent, this depends on the country context, but even at that, there are often varying results within a country. The ROAR 2010 reports on gender achievements, which are very limited, apart from elements of women's participation (it is not clear how much change this represents, as there appears to be no baseline).[35] Most of the reports are on strategies or actions still to be initiated. Still, reporting represents a commitment to keeping gender on the agenda.

The most consistent and positive results have been achieved in the area of the MDGs which, to varying degrees, have improved the incorporation and analysis of disaggregated data. This represents potential for improving gender equality since it collects and monitors data on gender issues, as well as sex-disaggregated data on a range of issues that can then be analysed with a gender perspective. As it is incorporated into national systems, this information should be useful for a range of policy decisions. The next important step would be to ensure that this data is used in all policy dialogue. This does not always happen. A case in point is the Samoa poverty reduction approach: the MDG indicators are improved, but the integrated framework and the PSSF fail to take gender into account at all. The ultimate result expected of a mainstreaming process is that gender be addressed in a project specific manner throughout the programme. This result is still a long way off.

UNDP and other UN members have put considerable emphasis on the joint UN Gender Working Group which has been particularly successful in promoting and supporting actions in line with the campaign UNITE against violence against women in the region. The UNCT RC report for 2010 indicates that broader integration of gender will be prioritized in the new UNDAF.

At the MCO levels, both offices developed gender strategies in 2007-2008. These strategies represent an important step in promoting and mainstreaming gender equality. However, results are still few.

The strategies could be considerably facilitated by the preparation of country-specific gender analyses, which is proposed in the Fiji document, but has yet to be implemented. A context-specific analysis should provide a shared understanding of the key obstacles and opportunities for greater gender equality, identify key institutions and allies, identify nationally significant indicators for promoting women's strategic interests,[36] and provide baseline information against which to monitor progress.[37] As it is, the strategy seems to be an action plan without clearly defined expected results.

At the project level, there is little analysis – even in cases where it was specified as a project output such as the SLM projects in seven of the Fiji MCO countries, the CCSDP in the four Samoa MCO countries – it has not been done. In the latter case, the analysis was to have served the whole MCO programme in the four countries.

Without clearly defined expected results and baseline information, it is impossible to evaluate the progress towards results represented by the information provided in the ROAR.

---

35 Due to evaluation logistic limitations, it was not possible to visit/address all of the individual gender activities. From an evaluation perspective, it is difficult to assess them given that strategies are not results based, but rather are activity based, and there is generally little baseline information.

36 Projects targeting women as beneficiaries or in relief projects are likely to address women's practical needs, which is valid, but may have no impact on the state of gender relations.

37 According to comments from the MCO, there was considerable analysis involved in developing the strategy. However, an explicit analysis is necessary to 1) provide a framework for monitoring and assessing results, and 2) for sharing with existing or new staff, partners and other stakeholders who so not share the same level of understanding.

In the case of Samoa, it was reported that channeling relief funds to women following the tsunami was an efficient way to get things done. This involves women and may help to meet their practical needs, but it does not necessarily empower women or contribute to greater equality – and it just might make their workload intolerable. However, it is also reported that this experience in project management changed attitudes by raising respect from male chiefs and could be built on in terms of political participation. This represents an opportunity that could easily be overlooked, or not acted on.[38] The same impact has not been noted in other emergency responses, and perhaps is a result of the special attention paid to gender in this case. Through the initiative of the protection cluster a longitudinal study was carried out that looked at impact on women, and integrated findings into early recovery response. Capacity to 'build back better' after a disaster should include identifying opportunities to promote women's empowerment.

The general weakness in gender may be due to the following factors:

- Beyond cases where equal participation of men and women are required, there is a general absence of any specific gender results, making it extremely difficult to monitor and assess gender achievements.

- Project-level staff does not appear to have any training, support or strategies for creatively addressing national level resistance to promoting gender equality, which may be expressed in direct or indirect ways.

- There is a great emphasis on the importance of maintaining and strengthening local traditions, even when these are discriminatory and excluding, not only of women, but of youth.

- Demand from countries in the region is not very high – except from the women's sector in some cases.

- There are no gender specialists in the MCOs. Gender is the responsibility of a focal point, which also has a range of other responsibilities, and may not have sufficient gender experience or expertise. In the Pacific Centre there are a number of gender specialists in the team although it just so happens that there is no specific post.

- Tools available, such as the gender strategy and the gender checklist in Samoa MCO, do not appear to be regularly used. In addition, they assume that the user has a good understanding of gender issues.

UNDP strategies and the UN Gender Working Group represent important initiatives to integrate gender into UNDP programmes. They have potential to have a significant impact if they manage to create:

- a shared analysis of gender equality issues at the national level that will identify strategic opportunities in all four thematic areas.

- clear, specific gender equality results, baseline and monitoring capacity

- an understanding of the role of men as well as women in promoting gender equality

- commitment of adequate human and financial resources.

5.4.3 CAPACITY DEVELOPMENT

Capacity development, along with policy development, is defined by the UNDAF as its 'main tenets' and the areas where it can have 'the greatest impact'. UNDP CPAPs generally stress the importance of capacity building at the national level. Although capacity development is considered an essential underpinning of UNDP activities, UNDP programming guidelines emphasize application of a comprehensive framework for

---

38 This result may have been planned or identified through special attention paid to gender. It was noted that the joint UN team action on the Samoa earthquake/tsunami response was good on gender – through the initiative of the protection cluster a longitudinal study was carried out that looked at impact on women, and integrated findings into early recovery response. Capacity to 'build back better' after a disaster should include identifying opportunities to promote women's empowerment.

capacity development in programme and project formulation. The framework consists of a three-tier strategy for capacity development starting with a higher enabling policy environment for capacity development, cascading down to developing institutional capacity at different levels in public sector (and civil societies) and integrating individual capacity development at the base through education, training and empowerment. Most UNDP projects tend to have capacity development intent, sometimes pronounced and other times implied or mute. In spite of the importance of this aspect of programming, there is no overall analysis or strategy[39] outlining the approaches to capacity development in the context of the Pacific. Very few projects also had any capacity assessment as part of the formulation. The Pacific region provides a series of challenges to capacity development, including small human resource bases, outmigration, and remote geographies. The evaluation team heard a number of times how projects stalled because a single key manager left his/her position and could not be quickly and effectively replaced. This has resulted in more active monitoring at the implementation level by UNDP staff, and a subsequent increased demand on MCOs resources resulting often in 'band-aid' approaches.

There is significant variation in these factors among the islands. The capacity issues of a relatively large country like Fiji are distinct from those of Niue, for example, with a population of less than 1,500. Relatively compact countries like Samoa do not face the administrative challenges of FS Micronesia or Palau with dispersed islands.

These challenges have long been recognized but not resolved. The UNDAF for Tuvalu in 2003-2007 analysed capacity issues in this micro country; the subregional UNDAF recognized capacity weakness as an obstacle. Most projects address the issue of capacity. The UNDAF mid-term evaluation notes that although capacity development is central to UNDP's strategy, the document says little about capacity except that it is a risk factor for a number of outcomes (the notable exception is strengthening data integrity at local level). The problem is persistent.

This is not to say that there are no good examples of successful capacity building. The Parliamentary Support project in Solomon Islands, for example, shows the value of a multi-faceted systemic approach to capacity development. In a number of cases (Samoa, Cook Islands, Vanuatu) there has been a significant improvement in national capacity to collect data at all levels, analyse it, select appropriate indicators to measure progress (especially relating to MDGs) and incorporate the findings into new national development strategies. In Cook Islands, Samoa, Niue, Nauru, Vanuatu and Tonga national capacities have been improved to assess climate vulnerabilities, generate climate scenarios and make policy-decisions for appropriate mitigation and adaptation measures. Through UNDP's support, similar work is underway in FS Micronesia, Kiribati, RMI and Tuvalu.

Samoa MCO's support through South-South Cooperation and Capacity Development Projects (SSCCDPs) over the past two decades in Samoa and Cook Islands has been key contributors to capacity development in Samoa. Samoa is now able to host South-South exchanges with other PICs. This fund has clearly been useful for the government capacity development through access to training, professional development and support of consultants. The SSCCDP for the Cook Islands funded an International UNV located in the Aid Management Division in the Ministry of Finance and Economic Management (MFEM) whose contributions to enhanced aid coordination is well documented. Inspired by the benefits, the Aid Management Division in Cook Islands is hiring a UN Coordination Desk Officer funded through their budget, to continue the work of the IUNV.

However, in spite of these successful examples of capacity building, a number of issues consistently recurred across the islands, with particular acuteness in the smaller and micro states.

---

39 The analysis is done on an ongoing basis at the CPAP level in order to address gaps.

The issues observed include:

- Small government departments and turnover of trained staff: Often projects depend on just one or two specialized staff, given the small size of many government departments. If they leave for another department at least the capacity is maintained in-country. In many cases, they migrate out of the country. Projects can be delayed by months with the departure of just one person.

- Participating in training and regional meetings (particularly related to GEF commitments) consumed enormous amounts of time that was not spent on normal work.

- Training seems to be the most common form of capacity building. Yet there has been little monitoring of the results of training, and how it contributed to institutional capacity.

- Training was often focused on capacity building for project management of UNDP systems (e.g., Prince, HACT, RBM) rather than what might be institutional priorities. This is a response to weaknesses identified by audits over the past two cycles.

- As capacity building was generally addressed in the context of a specific project, it usually addressed the needs of the project rather than the needs of the implementing institution. These needs are not necessarily the same. While any general management capacity will add to the national stock of expertise, it may not necessarily focus on the key capacity priorities of the country.

- Complex UNDP reporting systems and delays in responses or financial transfers often put extra burden on already small and stretched departments' capacities. Countries generally reported that these problems were greatly reduced when there was a UNDP or JPO person in country to link with the UNDP MCO.

There is an urgent need to review UNDP's approaches to capacity development, analysing achievements to date and lessons learned to produce an overall strategy for capacity development. The study should look at the inherent capacity issues in the partner countries – especially the smaller ones (Niue, Tokelau, Tuvalu, Cook Islands, and Nauru), as well as the extra burdens that UNDP programmes might place on these governments. It should clarify whether capacity building is in itself a priority for UNDP or whether it is a tool for ensuring proper management under NEX of UNDP programmes.

Among the elements identified to promote capacity development are:

- Approaching capacity development first from the needs of the implementing partner, not the project, or UNDP reporting processes.

- Taking a systems-wide approach, as was done in the Parliamentary Support project

- Taking into consideration the cultural norms and practices, and introducing acceptable mitigation measures, if necessary.

- Avoiding standalone projects that require separate personnel and resources to manage.

- Simplifying and aligning processes with national systems, where possible.

- Developing human resource strategies with partners that identify specific training and professional development needs, and gaps that can best be filled by some kind of outsourcing.

- One size does not fit all: Taking into account differences across the region, especially 1) size and human resource base, and 2) special relationships with either the USA or NZ that distort salary incentives and put competition for human resources on an international level.

- Monitoring capacity building results alongside project results, and incorporating lessons learned for future programmes.

- Hiring a national personnel (UNDP) or JPO in each country (most, but not all, already have one) and ensuring that monitoring and supporting a capacity development strategy is part of his/her responsibility. Their evolving role should be closely monitored, in terms of both workload and effectiveness.

- Addressing internal processes or inefficiencies in UNDP offices that might be generating extra work for national partners.

A special case should be made for capacity development of CSOs. In most countries, these have been identified as important for service delivery, data gathering and contribution to policy based on the relationship with their constituencies, and for their contribution to the development of democratic debate. Currently NGOs participate in UNDP programmes through such channels as the GEF SGP projects and certain MCO projects (such as civil society strengthening in Tonga) and through regional initiatives such as CPAD (Capacity building for Peace and Development).

5.5 MCO MANAGEMENT ISSUES

The evaluation team strongly felt that there are certain issues of management and programme oversight which clearly impinge on the efficiency and effectiveness of UNDP performance and achievement of results in the PICs. It also has implications for UNDP organizational setting in the Pacific in the context reaffirming UNDP's role and value added in the evolving regional architecture. The issue is elaborated below.

5.5.1 SUBSTANTIVE AND PROGRAMME MANAGEMENT SUPPORT TO THE COUNTRIES

During the country missions it emerged that there were demands for substantive and technical inputs from the project level which often were not met expeditiously by UNDP. The country respondents also indicated the need for support from UNDP in programme and financial management aspects. Relatively well-designed projects suffer from start-up and implementation delays due to lengthy approval processes, lengthy procurement processes for experts and consultants, and delays in financial transfers. Many of the projects visited lacked proper technical monitoring reports, of technical vetting or oversight on major outputs, or substantive facilitation of processes within the government. The government counterparts expected such inputs coming from UNDP.

However, it should be noted that the MCOs made efforts to address areas of weakness identified in the past, and jointly (with country) or individually coming up with ways to deal with its operational and budgetary constraints, which perhaps was inadequate or transitory due to financial and human resource constraints. The second issue to be reckoned with is the large number of projects undertaken by the MCOs. For example, 124 open projects for Fiji MCO alone works out to about 14 projects per country (high transaction costs and resource constraints). The important point is that to proceed beyond the status quo, there is a need to either increase budgetary resources for monitoring travel and technical support or coming up with alternative ways such as technical support arrangements with institutions in the region for project support or more deployment of people at the country level.

Based on interaction with the MCOs, the PC and the stakeholders across countries, the evaluation mission considers that the present division of labour between the MCOs (with focus on country programmes) and the Pacific Centre (on regional programmes) is not working seamlessly in delivering UNDP assistance to individual countries. If the focus is delivery of development results at the country level, then all the efforts of UNDP should be focused on servicing the country. The delivery of such services should be organized and managed based on the expertise and resources available in both the MCOs and the Pacific Centre.

The evaluation team also recognized that in recent years some progress has been made to address the issues of work planning and accountability between the MCOs and the Pacific Centre. At the programme level, Pacific Centre technical advisory support at the country level is guided primarily by what Fiji and Samoa MCOs have agreed with the relevant country. The Pacific Centre responds to requests for service via the relevant country office. As such, its work plan is driven by the priorities outlined in the relevant country work plans for the year. Such Pacific Centre technical support has been complemented by follow-up at the country level as part of regional advocacy work.

The leadership of MCOs and the Pacific Centre need to introduce a more seamless and efficient country demand management system through an institutional arrangement or mechanism between the MCOs and the Pacific Centre integrating, coordinating and sharing the responsibility of the provision of programme management and of specialist technical services. The mission observed good cooperation and understanding between the leaders of MCOs and the Pacific Centre, but somehow the integration of service provision has not yet reached a level delivering optimally to the best interest of PICs. The issue of relationship between the Pacific Centre and the MCOs has been dealt separately in the report of a high-level RBAP-sponsored review in 2009.

5.5.2 ORGANIZATION OF PROGRAMMES AND OFFICES

The above issue leads to another important question of whether UNDP has organized its programmes and offices in the Pacific in most effective ways to contribute to development results. UNDP has two Multi-Country Offices in Fiji and Samoa, one sub-office in Solomon Island, the Pacific Centre in Fiji and a host of Joint Country Presence offices (shared with UNICEF and UNFPA). The composition, skill levels, and capacity of the MCOs and the sub-offices vary substantially. Some country-level stakeholders suffer from confusion about the respective roles of the MCO and the Pacific Centre. There is an urgent need to establish clearer roles and responsibilities of the each UNDP units (MCOs and Pacific Centre) with clearer but flexible guidelines for integrated engagement for servicing the countries. The RBAP review mission (Hope Report) identified a number of intrinsic reasons such as competition, recognition, loss of identity and influence, which are considered inhibiting factors for effective coordination and functioning.

It would be pertinent to mention here that the feedback from governments, donors and civil society on services provided by the Pacific Centre point to a number of value-added dimensions and strengths: that it works well with partners; undertakes regional consultations; provides direct technical advice to governments upon request; and promotes regional cooperation and/or integration. Its efforts in many instances brought the governments, civil society organizations and donors together to coordinate their efforts and produce nationally owned solutions. A review of its research publications and ongoing works also confirms that it undertakes transnational research, pilot initiatives and advocacy relevant to the MDGs, from pro-poor macroeconomic and human development to democratic governance, gender equality and crisis prevention. The evaluation team received excellent feedback from the countries on the quality and promptness of technical and knowledge services from the Pacific Centre. All told, it is a veritable strength that should be leveraged fully by UNDP management to contribute to development effectiveness of the PICs.

Much can be achieved through an integration of the regional programmes of the Pacific Centre more closely with the country programmes, and an integrated approach to servicing the technical and knowledge needs of the countries. The technical and programme management skills and strengths of the Pacific Centre and the MCOs should converge to service the country demands under a unified oversight. This might change orientation and modality of providing services to the region by UNDP and can only be achieved through bold and coherent management decisions and follow-through.

A third dimension of strength is added by the new Country Presence Offices. This model received all round applause by the governments in that they are providing excellent facilitative and communication benefits. UNDP should consider leveraging them more with upgraded capacity training and delegation of routine programme responsibilities. The issue remains with the level of delegation for the Solomon Islands sub-office and the Country Presence Offices. Without a certain level of delegation, the staff there is deemed ineffective. Too much delegation has other associated risks. UNDP experience in other regions could provide good lessons.

In view of the UNDAF and the willingness of UN agencies to consolidate efforts through improved programming, some UN agencies raised the issue of UNDP's two offices in the subregion while all others had one. There have been reviews in the past on the effectiveness and efficiency of such an arrangement. Given the new architecture of field presence of the UN system in the Pacific, it would be appropriate for UNDP to have a deeper assessment of the efficacy of the present set-up and explore the possibility of smarter options.

Chapter 6
CONCLUSIONS AND RECOMMENDATIONS

6.1 CONCLUSIONS

In the Pacific, UNDP has consistently provided development assistance as a conscientious partner to support the development challenges of the PICs. It is serving a wide variety of countries with multi-faceted development needs. The UNDP MCOs face a daunting challenge of maximizing effectiveness and efficiency with many limitations of resources (both financial and human), capacity constraints and complexities of distance, spread of coverage, and diversity.

Conclusion 1: Development Results

Overall, UNDP in the Pacific has made important contributions during the period under review to meet the development challenges that the countries are facing. Good inroads have been made in mainstreaming and internalizing MDGs in the planning and budgetary processes of the countries. Substantial progress has been achieved in understanding poverty as a pressing development issue through policy and analytical research. Progress is also notable in some spheres of democratic governance. There is good achievement in the area of crisis prevention and recovery in terms of responding to immediate disaster and strengthening disaster management. Innovative and downstream approaches have shown good results in the area of energy and environment. Efforts and important national initiatives were supported in the area of gender equality with mixed success. Finally, capacity development was a built-in and cross-cutting strategy in project and programme interventions. The contribution in this sphere remains fraught with endemic challenges of brain drain, rotation within public service and out-migration. In many cases where the expected results have not been met or their achievements are delayed, this has been largely due to a combination of factors including those outside UNDP's control. With this qualification, UNDP has been generally effective in its contributions to the subregion.

Conclusion 2: Relevance

The four areas of outcome focus continue to be most relevant for the medium term with additional complementarities with downstream interventions and dispersal of efforts to sub-national, outer islands or depressed areas. UNDP interventions during the two programme periods addressed a subregional development agenda relevant to all PICs through an overarching strategic programme focus as a basis for individual country projects and initiatives. The programmes spanned from responding to most urgent challenges of disasters to supporting various spheres of longer term goals of democratic governance; from responding to macro issues of national poverty to provision of solar energy to households; from forging partnership with key national government agencies to regional organizations and bilateral donors to working hand in hand with downstream civil society organizations on local development initiatives. Operating effectively within this wide range of spheres and partners, UNDP demonstrated its ability for consistent strategic alignment of its activities, to be imaginative and responsive, and its agility of operating within a dynamic partnership environment.

To ensure better relevance and effectiveness, UNDP based on experience should consider differentiated strategy for interventions in smaller island countries (called micro states). Experience in the region has shown that relevance of the standard approach which has worked for most of the Pacific island countries is limited in the context of the so called micro states. The development needs of these countries require attention at downstream and local-level interventions. Service provision in micro states is always more costly and effort-intensive because of their thin government structures and lack of critical mass of trained people due to brain drain. In this context, the capacity infusion, project development and implementation modalities in these countries require looking at alternative approaches.

Conclusion 3: Effectiveness

Development results of UNDP interventions show a wide variance in terms of effectiveness. They varied from country to country, by areas of focus, by level of national preparedness, by level of resource and by degree of partnership with stakeholders The projects were generally well designed in a consultative way, but often suffered from delays in approval and start-up process. The responsibility for this is shared by both the national and the UNDP side. Implementation delays are a normal phenomenon in the Pacific with delays or inability in designating technical counterparts, in consultant recruitment process and erratic flow of required budget resource from UNDP's side. Many times, projects operate in a stand-alone existence outside the mainstream action or institutional structure of the government agency/ministry, which makes its eventual integration difficult.

Effectiveness in terms of progress towards outputs has been generally satisfactory and at times excellent, but progress towards outcome is more varied and difficult to ascertain. It was difficult to establish a proportionate link among the hierarchy of outcome statements in reference documents like the UNDAF, the MCPD, the CPAP and the project documents. Effectiveness in actualizing results has been much greater where the projects were driven by the government agency's priority and integrated within its current plan. Therefore, in future it would be imperative to ensure how the project has situated itself within the scheme of things in the department or the ministry. Synchronizing the project approval and implementation process with governments' ministry and sectoral plans would better ensure their effectiveness.

Overall, the attention to project-level technical monitoring and enhancing easy access by projects to UNDP's technical knowledge and support still remains an urgent necessity. Better acceptance of policy-level work and consideration by the government can be facilitated by technical quality assurance of processes and outputs by technically competent professionals. Project outputs with policy implications also require a momentum of substantive deliberation overtime with different levels in government. This requires qualified and articulate professionals in the subject area to be available periodically at the project level. UNDP can facilitate this by making its pool of expertise available at that level. Examples of such support can be found in areas of MDG support, poverty analysis, financial inclusion programme, integrated trade support, parliamentary strengthening, in environmental/climate adaptation plans. UNDP MCOs drawing on Pacific Centre services in many cases filled this requirement with excellent results. This means that provision of technical service to country level needs an integrated response system from UNDP (the MCO and the Pacific Centre)

Conclusion 4: Efficiency

Efficiency of programme management by UNDP over the two programme cycles has been mixed. Programmatic efficiency in terms of appropriate design, targeting stakeholders, distribution of focus and activities between upstream and downstream level, managing stakeholders, etc., were considered moderately satisfactory with some exceptions. Overambitious plans and unpredictable sources of funding at times caused initiatives to stall and face inefficiency.

The main issue of concern was managerial efficiency involving timeliness of approval of projects, timely procurement of inputs, and recruitment of technical experts/consultants, disbursement of funds. The perceptions from majority of the countries and counterparts were negative. Although fund disbursal has improved significantly over the years, the perception of inefficiencies remains. The approval of management and financial issues from the two MCOs for outlying country projects was mostly considered slow or sluggish. UNDP's procedures, regulations, paper trail, and reporting requirements are not always understood at project level. The geographical coverage and challenges of administering programmes in remote countries and locations, and the centralized nature of UNDP MCO administrations, leave the project offices with limited authority of resource allocation, recruitment and procurement. Sometimes weak competence of national project staff, staff turnover at national level and lack of handing over procedures also contribute to delays and inefficiencies. This limitation puts UNDP at a disadvantage in building a constructive relationship with state and local government authorities and CSOs, especially for projects on decentralization and area-based environment projects.

Efficiency of project management at the site level, especially at sub-national or outer island level, was weak. Late designation of counterparts, high turnover, lack of proper understanding of processes, lack of substance on the project are some of the chronic problems. Proper and regular monitoring and follow-up by UNDP could be instrumental in detecting and solving some of these issues. Some projects pointed out lack of creative solutions and inability to adapt to unanticipated changes by the project personnel also creates delays. However, high operational costs (travel, communications, etc.) limits UNDP monitoring to one per year (Northern Pacific) and twice, resources permitting, for most nearby countries – specifically for project management and monitoring. UNDP needs to consider more allocation for such purposes if the above issues are to be addressed.

There were also endemic rigidities in the NEX and NIM processes which may have been the cause of some delays. For the PICs, the amenability of applying NEX or NIM should be assessed carefully, considering the capacity constraints and based on criteria of efficiency, transaction costs and cost in terms implementation delays due to inadequate response capacity of the government apparatus. This issue requires to be raised at the headquarters policy level for requesting flexibility in specific cases.

High turnover in UNDP staff in the Samoa MCO and the sub-office in Solomon Islands is seen as limiting effectiveness and efficiency of projects, resulting in a negative image of organizational effectiveness. The frequent and sizeable staff turnover was pointed out as problematic by counterparts. This phenomenon not only delays but also at times interrupts smooth project implementation due to lack of or delayed action from UNDP. Stability in human resource is a sine qua non of good performance. While there may be valid reasons for such turnover, this issue needs to be analysed by UNDP to come up with some pragmatic and systemic solutions for the longer run.

The UN Joint Presence Offices have been applauded by the governments and they are already showing effectiveness. They are seen by the countries as facilitators of trouble-shooting, communications with the MCOs and logistics management for projects and missions by UN agencies. Their capacities may be leveraged even more in the future for programme support functions.

Conclusion 5: Sustainability

Greater sustainability was observed in projects that supported initiatives with strong national ownership and commitment backed by established national strategy and budgetary allocation. For example, UNDP support of the MDG process and its integration in national policy and planning enjoyed significant promise of longer sustainability. At the project level, sustainability has been affected by lack of attention to institutional integration, lack of adequate capacity development and preplanning of exit and sometimes external factors.

Positive experiences and potential of sustainability emerged in projects where there was close engagement with CSOs in managing resources and processes. This was backed by commitment to sustain the project benefits by local population groups. When downstream service-oriented projects or sustainable resource management projects are eventually handed over to CSOs or local institutions, they usually survive the test of time. The experiences have been solidified through CCSDP and SGP projects which had very strong CSO, NGO and popular interface. These experiences should be codified for use in the forthcoming programme cycle.

Capacity development goes beyond technical training and imparting skills to people. A systemic view and institutional approach helps better to ingrain capacities within the institution. An example of good practice is support to parliaments. These initiatives took a systemic view of work streams in parliament and tried to enhance the capacities in various ways, i.e., training, handbooks, and establishment of committee structure, record management systems and procedures. It proved to be effective and sustainable.

Different layers of institutions require a mix of support such as short-term technical interventions and long-term in situ technical capacity development. Given the focus of UNDP on reforms, it should consider longer term sustained support to those initiatives. One-off support to a longer term issue remains a tendency of UNDP.

Conclusion 6: Comparative Strength

UNDP leverage as a repository of global knowledge and development experience and a gateway to global network is underutilized. The opportunity is missed to leverage the joint strength of the MCOs and the Pacific Centre in a systematic and synchronized way to deliver best knowledge, capacity and technical substance at the country level. The intrinsic perceptive divide and lack of integrated management structure is identified as the main reason for less than optimal performance in this area.

UNDP's substantive niche and capacity to deliver is well recognized in policy-oriented poverty work, governance, crisis prevention and recovery. UNDP strength and knowledge for technical GEF project formulation and project management expertise is generally acknowledged by the governments and other stakeholders. In view of the increasing number of agencies with more technical clout crowding the area, UNDP needs to establish a specific niche for itself (beyond competence in project management support) in the area of environmental governance. This role will enable it to retain its role as one of the main development agencies in environment.

Conclusion 7: Promotion of UN values

The performance is satisfactory in terms of promotion of UN values. MDGs and poverty analysis work had good effect in the mindset of policy-makers in a number of countries. However, work on gender equality and human rights-based approaches require more attention and follow-through at project-level work. Capacity for gender analysis and integration of gender dimension require attention in-house and should be a dimension in performance management system. At a macro level, capacity development would be greatly enhanced by an overall country- or ministry-level strategy for capacity development, to enhance the potential for interventions to contribute to national priorities. That can be supplemented by a practical strategy for capacity assessment and development at project formulation stage and monitoring during implementation.

Conclusion 8: Partnership and coordination

UNDP has maintained a good level of positive and useful partnership across the governments, donors, regional organizations and civil society organizations. The new frontier of partnership with CSOs in downstream work in civic education, environment, sustainable livelihood and development, decentralization needs to be leveraged for greater results at local level. The partnership for work with the regional organizations requires a coordinated strategy with other UN system organizations in the Pacific. Instead of a perception (which may be mutual) of competing in some areas, the strategy should focus on leveraging comparative and value-added strength of UNDP in promoting effectiveness and sustainability of national programmes.

The work in UN coordination seemed to be effective with an excellent interactive and willing environment. The UNDAF framework has given a window of opportunity to bring the UN system strength to support development in the Pacific. But not much work was evident in promoting the effort in joint programming or integrated country-oriented programming, an area which should be a natural next step for the UN system.

6.2 RECOMMENDATIONS

Recommendation 1: Programme focus

The four outcome areas with gender equality as a cross-cutting theme continue to be most relevant for the PICs. Hence, emphasis for the next programme cycle should be continued and consolidated in those areas. Experiences on some of those areas have started generating nationally embedded endeavours. Policy analysis and programme intervention support in the areas of poverty, employment, sustainable livelihood, food security, governance (parliament, electoral assistance, civic education, and decentralization), private sector, environment and climate change, and crisis prevention should continue to receive priority attention.

Recommendation 2: Programme strategy

UNDP's emphasis of work at central and policy level should be balanced with opportunities for work at downstream and outreach level with CSOs and communities in view of good experiences of effectiveness and results observed during the current cycle. This is particularly suitable in smaller islands. Downstream work should be used to inform policy making.

A differentiated programme strategy and approach could be considered for smaller island countries due to their specific situation, high unit cost of delivery and inherent capacity constraints. The development needs and interventions should be assessed based on the nature of the country. For example, options could be pursued for fewer and more integrated projects to reduce management workload, special measures for meeting capacity gaps, and joint/shared programme frameworks with other agencies.

A coherent strategy should be strengthened and implemented for mainstreaming of gender equality. It should include a shared gender analysis at the regional level and at the national level. The analyses should assess priorities and opportunities for promoting gender equality and/or women's empowerment that should inform UNDP strategy. The project formulations must include a gender analysis for use in project management. Programme staff should have access to support and resources in this regard.

The capacity development intent and content of projects should be made explicit at formulation stage with a detailed capacity assessment and statement of a strategy for capacity development which should be monitored and accounted for in progress reports.

Recommendation 3: Project cycle management

UNDP should accord priority and adequate technical support to this aspect. Project formulation should be addressed in a technically competent fashion. A thorough appraisal of the government's priority, the project's embeddedness in institutional context and capacity, should be undertaken during formulation to include all aspects.

Country Demand Management for substantive and technical support: Introduce a regime of organized country demand management in programming with a tight management oversight to address issues emerging at country project level and time-bound response system. UNDP should intensify conducting regular project management monitoring of progress. More importantly, it should introduce technical monitoring through quality assurance support of important products of the projects. The difference between the two types of monitoring should be understood clearly. Technical professionals services should be drawn from the Pacific Centre, if available, or from outside if necessary for this purpose. Monitoring should identify areas or products which require higher level dialogue and engagement within the government and policy makers. This continued engagement with professional inputs is essential to ensure effectiveness of project outputs.

Monitoring and evaluation: Introduce a more thorough and disciplined monitoring and evaluation system as part of wider management strategy. A system of holding agenda-based periodic tripartite review meetings could be introduced coinciding with monitoring visits to countries/projects. Monitoring of activity schedules, outputs, progress towards outcomes and project/programme finances should be carried out and recorded as part of an institutional system. This documented information is essential as a base for monitoring and evaluation. Project and outcome evaluations should be planned, monitored and carried out with due diligence with clear accountability assigned to programme staff and management.

Recommendation 4

Efficiency issues should be addressed on a number of fronts:

- **Choice of implementation mode should be guided by the country situation rather than corporate prescription of UNDP.** The feasibility and efficiency of working with NEX and DEX modality should be studied in each case to choose the appropriate modality. If required, a well-argued case for flexibility in small islands should be made by the MCO to UNDP headquarters based on efficiency and results considerations.

- **Reasons should be identified for the trend in delays in approvals.** If some systemic and process prescriptions require more time, provide it in the planning phase and avoid unrealistic planning targets at the outset.

- **More flexible HR modalities or options for project level recruitment should be introduced.** Introduce retainer contracts, periodic technical support from institutions in the region, where recruitment of longer term technical personnel is proving difficult.

- **The issue of delays in fund transfers to projects should be addressed.** The system of transfer should work with equal efficiency in all cases, unless there are explainable constraints. At the project level appropriate training should be imparted in cash flow planning and management.

Recommendation 5

Production of a periodic subregional Human Development Report should be considered to facilitate advocacy work on sensitive issues in the subregion and also to provide added support for promotion and compliance with UN values.

Recommendation 6

Connect, integrate, and infuse UNDP's global knowledge and solution to Pacific project-level work. The Pacific Centre's comparative advantage in terms of its current work, focus and proven knowledge management competence should be coordinated with the MCOs' country demand management system. UNDP's comparative advantage as repository of global knowledge and experience requires greater application at the programme and project levels. This would also enhance quality of project-level development work. This require systematic and intentionality in application.

Recommendation 7

Introduce an institutional oversight system that would enable the MCOs and Pacific Centre to consolidate the organization's strength to deliver better quality development assistance. The performance of the current rules of engagement should be reviewed and applied with regular oversight by the senior management of the MCOs and the Pacific Centre. A dedicated participatory management deliberation between the MCOs, the Pacific Centre and the Regional Bureau for Asia and the Pacific is recommended to seriously explore potential options and follow it up with bold decisions to implement all consequential changes such as integrated work plan, clear decision-making structure and accountability and financial management. If the distinctive UNDP aspect of global knowledge infusion in programmes is not made visible and useful, its position as a value-adding partner to the PICs may be undermined.

Annex 1

TERMS OF REFERENCE

INTRODUCTION

The Evaluation Office (EO) of the United Nations Development Programme (UNDP) conducts evaluations called Assessments of Development Results (ADRs) to capture and demonstrate evaluative evidence of UNDP's contributions to development results at the country level, as well as the effectiveness of UNDP's strategy in facilitating and leveraging national effort for achieving development goals. ADRs are carried out within the overall provisions contained in the UNDP Evaluation Policy,[40] following the methodology developed by the EO for ADRs.

The purpose of an ADR is to:

- Provide substantive support to the Administrator's accountability function in reporting to the Executive Board
- Support greater UNDP accountability to national stakeholders and partners in the programme countries
- Serve as a means of quality assurance for UNDP interventions at the country level
- Contribute to learning at corporate, regional and country levels

The ADR in the Pacific Island Countries (ADR Pacific) will study UNDP's contributions to development results made during the current and previous programme cycles 2003-2007 and 2008-2012, with more attention given to the recent contributions, in 14 Pacific island countries, namely: Cook Islands, Federated States of Micronesia, Fiji, Kiribati, Nauru, Niue, Palau, the Republic of the Marshall Islands, Samoa, Solomon Islands, Tokelau, Tonga, Tuvalu, and Vanuatu. It will be conducted in 2011 so as to make inputs to the preparation of new multi-country programmes that start from 2013, which are to be approved by UNDP's Executive Board in 2012.

DEVELOPMENT CONTEXT

The Pacific is a geographically vast, culturally and ecologically diverse and, in human development terms, highly variable region.[41] Middle-income countries function alongside five Least Developed Countries (LDCs)[42] in the region, and the Millennium Development Goal indicators in rural areas or on the outer islands of many countries are well below national average and equivalent to any LDC.

Societies in the Pacific have been experiencing dramatic social, economic and environmental transformations over the past decades. Governance systems have, in general, struggled to meet the human development needs of their populations, and often co-exist uneasily alongside traditional forms of governance. A myriad of factors have led to political instability and civil conflict in several countries in recent years. Human rights are not widely understood, gender inequality is pervasive, and half of the population of the region is under 25 and faces limited social, economic and political opportunities.

Subsistence production dominates the economic life of most of the region's people, but urbanization,

---

[40] <www.undp.org/eo/documents/Evaluation-Policy.pdf>
[41] The description of the challenges here is derived from the United Nations Development Assistance Framework 2008-2013.
[42] Kiribati, Samoa, Solomon Islands, Tuvalu and Vanuatu.

migration, high population growth, declining rural productivity, globalization, and small/slow-growing formal economies, among other factors, are transforming economies around the region. Poverty is a problem: an average of one in four households has an income below national basic needs poverty lines in the region.

Population growth and economic changes are putting strain on the natural environment on which most people depend. The rich biodiversity of the region is threatened through contact with humans, resource exploitation and pollution, and Pacific people and ecology are particularly vulnerable to natural disasters and climate change. Each of these problems has human rights and gender dimensions.

Pacific island countries are also active in promoting development through regional cooperation. At the Pacific Islands Forum, of which the countries are members or observers, the Governments endorsed in 2005 the 10-year Pacific Plan with a view to enhancing and stimulating economic growth, sustainable development, good governance and security for Pacific countries through regionalism.

UNDP RESPONSE TO DEVELOPMENT CHALLENGES IN THE PACIFIC (2003-2011)

UNDP supports Pacific island countries under three programmes approved by the Executive Board of UNDP, namely:

- Multi-country programme, operated by the Multi-Country Office (MCO) located in Fiji, covering Federated States of Micronesia, Fiji, Kiribati, Nauru, Palau, the Republic of the Marshall Islands, Solomon Islands, Tonga Tuvalu, and Vanuatu.

- Multi-country programme, operated by the Multi-Country Office located in Samoa, covering Cook Islands, Niue, Samoa and Tokelau.

- Asia-Pacific regional programme which includes projects and activities supporting Pacific island countries individually or collectively, operated by the Asia-Pacific Regional Centre in large part through its Pacific Centre (PC).

To operationalize these programmes, UNDP enters into an agreement to implement Country Programme Action Plan (CPAP) with the Government of each country.

Through these programmes, UNDP provides policy advice, capacity development, advocacy and other operational activities with a view to facilitating the attainment of Millennium Development Goals, poverty reduction, democratic governance, sustainable use of environment and energy, prevention of and recovery from conflicts and disaster, and other goals of UNDP such as gender equality.

For the current programme cycle of 2008-2012, the United Nations system has established a common strategic framework, the United Nations Development Assistance Framework (UNDAF), to support all 14 Pacific island countries served by the two UN Country Teams in Fiji and Samoa.[43] UNDP's two multi-country programmes operated by the MCOs in Fiji and Samoa were developed under this framework. In the previous programme cycle 2002-2007, however, the approach was not as consistent: UNDAF was developed only for the country of Samoa, which also had a separate country programme apart from the multi-country programme covering the three other countries supported by the MCO in Samoa.

UNDP in the Pacific works predominantly in four areas: poverty reduction, including pro-poor national development plans and strategies aligned to the MDGs; democratic governance and human rights, which includes working on

---

43 FAO, ILO, OHCHR, UNAIDS, UNESCAP, UNDP (including the Pacific Centre), UNESCO, UNFPA, UNICEF, UNIFEM, UNHCR, UNOCHA, UNOPS, WHO and WMO. More UN agencies are expected to join the UNCTs in Fiji and Samoa, such as IFAD and UNEP.

Table A1. Fiji and Samoa MCOs Programme Expenditure by Practice Area (2004-2010, US$ Thousands)		
Practice Area	Fiji MCO 2004-2010 Expenditure	Samoa MCO 2004-2010 Expenditure
Achieving MDGs and Reducing Poverty	16,971	2,580
Fostering Democratic Governance	38,831	2,353
Environment Sustainable Development	46,296	19,378
Not entered	7,468	1,331
Total	117,818	26,209

Source: UNDP Atlas Executive Snapshot, 22 February 2011

principles of good leadership and accountability, the protection of human rights and the support for enhanced participation in decision making, as well as decentralization; crisis prevention and recovery, which includes disaster risk management and responses to humanitarian crises; and environment and sustainable development.

The total programme expenditure of UNDP of the MCO in Fiji, covering 10 countries, for the years 2004 to 2010 was US$117,818,000 and of the MCO in Samoa, covering four countries, for the same period was US$26,209,000. Table A1 presents a consolidated expenditure by both MCOs. Tables A2 and A3 provide a detail of programme expenditure by country by practice area (see pp. 85 and 86, respectively).

In order to enhance their assistance to individual countries, UNDP, UNICEF and UNFPA offices initiated in 2006 the Pacific UN Joint Presence. Currently, in eight countries of Solomon Islands, Kiribati, Vanuatu, Federated States of Micronesia, Nauru, the Marshall Islands, Palau and Tuvalu, one of the agencies has established a presence that also acts on behalf of the other agencies.

OBJECTIVES OF THE EVALUATION

The objectives of the ADR are:
- To provide an independent assessment of the progress or lack of, towards the expected outcomes envisaged in the UNDP programming documents. Where appropriate, the ADR will also highlight unexpected outcomes (positive or negative) and missed opportunities;
- To provide an analysis of how UNDP has positioned itself to add value in response to national needs and changes in the national development context;
- To present key findings, draw key lessons, and provide a set of clear and forward-looking options for the management to make adjustments in the current strategy and next Multi-Country Programme Documents.

SCOPE OF THE EVALUATION AND SPECIAL AREAS OF INTEREST

The ADR will review UNDP contribution to development results in the Pacific island countries under its two most recent multi-country programmes (2003-2007 and 2008-2012), as well as the parts of UNDP's Asia Pacific Regional Programme relevant to the achievement of national development results in these countries.

It will assess its contribution to the national effort in addressing its development challenges, encompassing social, economic and political spheres. It will assess key results, specifically outcomes – anticipated and unanticipated, positive and negative, intentional and unintentional – and will cover UNDP assistance funded from both core and non-core resources.

Table A2. Fiji MCO Programme Expenditure by Practice Area (2004-2010, US$ Thousands)

Practice Area	Fiji MCO Budget	Fiji MCO Expenditure
Not Entered	11,364	7,468
Achieving MDGs and Reducing Poverty	25,904	16,971
Fostering Democratic Governance	55,045	38,831
Energy and Environment for Sustainable Development	68,514	46,296
Crisis Prevention and Recovery	14,660	8,244
Total	**175,495**	**117,818**

Practice Area	Fiji Budget	Fiji Expenditure	Micronesia (FSM) Budget	Micronesia (FSM) Expenditure	Kiribati Budget	Kiribati Expenditure
Not Entered	4,544	3,149	77	42	285	209
Achieving MDGs and Reducing Poverty	8,135	5,451	67	44	0	0
Fostering Democratic Governance	20,206	14,617	0	0	1,296	1,013
Energy and Environment for Sustainable Development	30,099	20,959	840	305	974	634
Crisis Prevention and Recovery	6,030	3,087	0	0	0	0
Total	**69,014**	**47,263**	**984**	**391**	**2,557**	**1,857**

Practice Area	Marshall Islands Budget	Marshall Islands Expenditure	Nauru Budget	Nauru Expenditure	Palau Budget	Palau Expenditure
Not Entered	164	52	32	24	118	45
Achieving MDGs and Reducing Poverty	807	395	477	365	404	168
Fostering Democratic Governance	433	269	0	0	0	0
Energy and Environment for Sustainable Development	263	150	163	105	400	260
Crisis Prevention and Recovery	0	0	0	0	0	0
Total	**1,667**	**866**	**672**	**494**	**921**	**474**

Practice Area	Solomon Islands Budget	Solomon Islands Expenditure	Tonga Budget	Tonga Expenditure	Tuvalu Budget	Tuvalu Expenditure
Not Entered	226	144	5,446	3,665	145	65
Achieving MDGs and Reducing Poverty	2,133	1,441	12,023	7,864	601	358
Fostering Democratic Governance	5,247	3,260	27,182	19,159	444	366
Energy and Environment for Sustainable Development	846	322	33,585	22,735	538	245
Crisis Prevention and Recovery	1,300	1,035	7,330	4,122	0	0
Total	**9,753**	**6,203**	**85,568**	**57,548**	**1,731**	**1,035**

Source: UNDP Atlas Executive Snapshot. 22 February 2011

The evaluation has two main components: the analysis of the UNDP's contribution to development results through its programme outcomes and the strategy and positioning it has taken. For each component, the ADR will present its findings and assessment according to the set criteria provided below. Further elaboration of the criteria will be found in the 'ADR Manual 2011'.

Table A3. Samoa MCO Programme Expenditure by Practice Area (2004-2010, US$ Thousands)

	Samoa MCO		Samoa	
Practice Area	Budget	Expenditure	Budget	Expenditure
Not Entered	3,431	1,331	2,848	1,122
Achieving MDGs and Reducing Poverty	4,758	2,580	4,327	2,332
Fostering Democratic Governance	3,642	2,353	2,572	1,832
Energy and Environment for Sustainable Development	30,728	19,378	27,843	17,846
Crisis Prevention and Recovery	894	567	786	558
Total	43,453	26,209	38,376	23,690

	Cook Islands		Niue		Tokelau	
Practice Area	Budget	Expenditure	Budget	Expenditure	Budget	Expenditure
Not Entered	380	156	93	50	110	3
Achieving MDGs and Reducing Poverty	75	0	123	58	233	190
Fostering Democratic Governance	255	135	495	289	320	97
Energy and Environment for Sustainable Development	654	425	1,019	605	1,212	502
Crisis Prevention and Recovery	0	0	20	4	88	5
Total	1,364	716	1,750	1,006	1,963	797

Source: UNDP Atlas Executive Snapshot. 22 February 2011

UNDP'S CONTRIBUTION BY THEMATIC/PROGRAMMATIC AREAS

Analyses will be made on the contribution of UNDP to development results in Pacific through its programme activities. The analyses will be presented by thematic/programme areas and according to the following criteria:[44] relevance; effectiveness; efficiency; and sustainability.

Within the analyses above, and wherever applicable, particular attention will be paid to UNDP's effectiveness in promoting capacity development, and in using South-South cooperation, partnerships for development, and coordination of UN and other development assistance.

UNDP'S POSITIONING AND STRATEGIES

The positioning and strategies of UNDP are analysed both from the perspective of the organization's mandate[45] and the development needs and priorities in the countries. This would entail systematic analyses of UNDP's place and niche within the development and policy space in the Pacific, as well as strategies used by UNDP to maximize its contribution through adopting relevant strategies and approaches. The following criteria will be applied: relevance and responsiveness; exploiting comparative strengths; and promoting UN values from human development perspective.

---

44   If the assessments on efficiency and sustainability are found to be rather common across the thematic areas, the evaluation team may choose to present them in one place across thematic areas in order to avoid repetitions and enhance the readability of the report. Also, the ADR does not require presentation and examination of all the projects and activities; a representative sample of them could be used to illustrate findings as appropriate.

45   For UNDP's Strategic Plan, see <www.undp.org/execbrd/pdf/dp07-43Rev1.pdf>.

The ADR in the Pacific will cover all support provided by UNDP to the 14 Pacific island countries through its multiple programmes during the programme cycles of 2003-2007 and 2008-2012, while giving more attention to the ongoing programme.

KEY EVALUATION QUESTIONS AND EVALUATION CRITERIA

The fundamental questions to be examined in this evaluation are:

- Whether UNDP has played the most relevant role in assisting the PICs to address their own development challenges, based on the comparative strength that UNDP brings into the country;

- Whether UNDP rendered such assistance in a most effective, efficient and sustainable manner, and to what extent UNDP's assistance yielded development results; and

- Whether UNDP has responded appropriately to the evolving country and international situations by transforming its role and approaches.

Further, given the country context, the ADR Pacific should pay particular attention to the following aspects:

- Whether UNDP has most effectively cooperated with regional cooperation mechanisms, such as the Pacific Islands Forum, and with other development partners making contributions in the subregion;

- Whether the way UNDP supported capacity development efforts in the Pacific has been the most adequate for the challenges faced by small developing island states;

- Whether the way UNDP has organized its programmes and offices in the Pacific has been the most effective and efficient ways to contribute to development results in the Pacific island countries, also taking into account the Pacific UN Joint Presence initiative and the collaborative effort by the UN system as a whole in the subregion.

EVALUATION METHODS AND APPROACHES

The evaluation team will use a multiple-method approach. For data collection, that will entail the use of primary and secondary sources, using interviews, focus groups, project/field visits, direct observation or surveys. The evaluation team will make extensive use of documents and administrative records and will conduct desk reviews and meta-analysis as deemed appropriate to respond to the evaluation questions.

The evaluation team will use a variety of methods to ensure that the data is valid, including through triangulation. All the findings must be supported by evidence and validated through consulting multiple sources of information. The evaluation team is required to use an appropriate tool (e.g., an evaluation matrix to present findings from multiple sources) to show that all the findings are validated.

The evaluation team will make explicit the approach taken to qualitative data analysis. Working with qualitative data usually entails three processes: data reduction, data display, and deriving conclusions. The three processes are not necessarily sequential and may often overlap. Fully applying qualitative data collection and analysis tools can be a labour-intensive task. However, discipline in data-gathering and organization is a realistic goal for the ADR.

A strong participatory approach, involving a broad range of stakeholders, will be taken in the evaluation. The ADR will organize a reference group with representatives of the 14 Pacific Island Countries to orient the conduct and design of the evaluation. These stakeholders would include Government representatives, civil-society organizations, and private-sector representatives.

PRINCIPLES AND GUIDELINES

The ADR will be conducted in adherence to the Norms and the Standards[46] and the ethical Code of Conduct[47] established by the United Nations Evaluation Group (UNEG), as well as to UNDP's Evaluation Policy. All those engaged in designing, conducting and managing evaluation activities should conduct high-quality work guided by professional standards and ethical and moral principles. The integrity of evaluation is especially dependent on the ethical conduct of key actors in the evaluation. Evaluators are expected to demonstrate independence, impartiality, credibility and avoid any potential conflict of interest.

EVALUATION PROCESS

PHASE 1: PREPARATION

The EO will set up the terms of reference in consultation with key stakeholders, and establish the evaluation team. The EO will also undertake a preliminary research to prepare for the evaluation, and conduct a workshop for the team to understand the scope, the process, the approach and the methodology of the ADR.

PHASE 2: PRELIMINARY RESEARCH AND EVALUATION DESIGN

Evaluation design: Inception report – Based on the preparatory work by the EO and other information and materials obtained from the Governments, UNDP MCOs/PC and other sources, the evaluation team will develop the evaluation plan and submit it as an inception report. The evaluation plan should include:

- Brief overview of key development challenges, national strategies and UN/UNDP response to contextualize evaluation questions
- Specific evaluation questions for each evaluation criteria (as defined in the ADR Manual)
- Methods to be used and sources of information to be consulted in addressing each set of evaluation questions
- Preliminary hypotheses, if any, reached from the desk study for evaluation questions, with an indication of the information source (e.g., an evaluation report) that led to the hypothesis
- Selection of projects/activities to be examined in depth
- Plan for visits to project/field activity sites

PHASE 3: DATA COLLECTION AND ANALYSIS

Data collection – In terms of data collection, the evaluation team will use a multiple-method approach that could include document reviews, workshops, group and individual interviews, project/field visits and surveys. The set of methods for each evaluation criteria and questions should be defined in the inception report to be prepared by the evaluation team.

- The evaluation team should establish a schedule of its activities in consultation with UNDP EO and MCOs/PC. The field visits and observations should normally be arranged through the MCOs. The schedule may need to be detailed to ensure the data collection covers adequately the number of countries and issues under evaluation.
- The team will collect data according to the evaluation plan defined in the inception report, inter alia, by conducting interviews (in person and teleconferences), organizing focus group meetings, conducting surveys, and collecting further documentary evidences. Furthermore, in order to identify key development challenges of the country, the evaluation team may conduct interviews and consultations beyond those involved directly or indirectly in UNDP country programme.

---

46 <www.uneval.org/normsandstandards/index.jsp?doc_cat_source_id=4>
47 <www.uneval.org/papersandpubs/documentdetail.jsp?doc_id=102>

- During the data collection phase, the team may start the validation of emerging hypothesis and findings to facilitate the process and to ensure all of its findings are well supported.

Data analysis – The evaluation team will analyse the data collected to reach preliminary assessments, conclusions and recommendations.

- Once the data is collected, the evaluation team should dedicate collectively some time (up to one week) to its analysis. The task manager will join the team during this phase to assist in the analysis and validation.

- The outcome of the data analysis will be preliminary assessments for each evaluation criterion/question, general conclusions to answer key questions and provide overarching findings from the analysis, and strategic and operational recommendations.

- Once the preliminary assessments, conclusions and recommendations are thus formulated, the evaluation team will debrief UNDP MCOs/PC and the Reference Group to obtain feedback so as to avoid factual inaccuracies and/or misinterpretation.

PHASE 4: DRAFTING AND REVIEWS

First draft and the quality assurance – The evaluation team will further analyse information collected and incorporate the initial feedback from debriefing sessions. The team leader will coordinate the preparation of the first draft, and submit it to the EO. The first draft will be accepted by the EO, after revisions if necessary, when it is in compliance with the terms of reference, the ADR Manual and other established guidelines, and satisfies quality standards. The draft is also subject to a quality assurance process through external reviews.

Second draft and the verification and stakeholder comments – The first draft will be revised by the team leader with a support from other team members as required, to incorporate the feedback from the internal and external review process. Once satisfactory revisions to the draft are made, it becomes the second draft. The second draft will be forwarded by the EO to (a) UNDP MCOs/PC and Regional Bureau for Asia and Pacific (RBAP) and (b) Governments through the Reference Group, for factual verification and comments. The team leader will revise the second draft accordingly, while preparing an audit trail that indicates changes that are made to the draft, and submit it as the final draft. The EO may request further revisions before accepting it as the final draft if it considers necessary.

STAKEHOLDER PARTICIPATION

Stakeholder workshop – A stakeholder workshop will be organized to present preliminary findings, conclusions and recommendations to a wide range of stakeholders, and to obtain their feedback to be incorporated in the evaluation report.

PHASE 5: FOLLOW-UP

Management response – UNDP RBAP will prepare a management response based on inputs from the MCOs to the ADR, and will be responsible for monitoring and overseeing the implementation of follow-up actions in the Evaluation Resource Centre.[48]

Communication – The ADR report and brief will be widely distributed in both hard and electronic versions. The evaluation report will be made available to UNDP Executive Board by the time of approving the new multi-country programme documents. It will be widely distributed by UNDP and the members of the Reference Group to stakeholders in the country and at UNDP headquarters, to evaluation outfits of other international organizations, and to evaluation societies and research institutions in the

---

48 <erc.undp.org/>

region. The report and the management response will be published on the UNDP website.[49]

THE EVALUATION TEAM

The EO will compose an independent evaluation team to undertake the ADR. The team will be constituted of four members:

- team leader, with overall responsibility for providing guidance and leadership for conducting the ADR, and in preparing and revising draft and final reports;
- three team specialists, who will support the team leader and provide the expertise in specific subject areas of the evaluation, and may be responsible for drafting relevant parts of the report;
- research assistant in the EO who will be responsible for collecting the preliminary programme and financial documentation of UNDP in the Pacific.

The task manager of UNDP EO designated for ADR Pacific will also participate in the evaluation as a team member to the extent appropriate and feasible.

Qualifications

The team leader must satisfy the following qualifications:

- have a solid understanding of evaluation methodologies relevant to the ADR in Pacific, backed up by a proven expertise of research in social science;
- have a good understanding of the workings of the government, development assistance and UN/UNDP in particular;
- have a sound knowledge of development issues and challenges in Pacific in the areas relevant to the work of UNDP;
- have proven leadership and presentation skills in evaluation or research projects.

The team specialists must satisfy the following qualifications:

- have a good understanding of evaluation methodologies relevant to ADR in Pacific, and/or a proven expertise of research in social science relevant for the evaluation;
- have a sound knowledge of development issues and challenges, as well as the government policies, at least in one subject area relevant to the work of UNDP, and/or the sound knowledge of the workings of UN/UNDP.

To avoid conflict of interest, the members of the team should not have engaged in the design or implementation of the regional or multi-country programmes in question.

MANAGEMENT ARRANGEMENTS

UNDP EVALUATION OFFICE (EO)

UNDP EO will conduct the ADR. Its task manager will provide overall management of and technical backstopping to the evaluation. The task manager will set the terms of reference for the evaluation, select the evaluation team, receive the inception report, provide guidance to the conduct of evaluation, organize feedback sessions and a stakeholder meeting, receive the first draft of the report and decide on its acceptability, and manage the review and follow-up processes. The task manager will also support the evaluation team in understanding the scope, the process, the approach and the methodology of the ADR, provide ongoing advice and feedback to the team for quality assurance, and assist the team leader in finalizing the report. The EO will meet all costs directly related to the conduct of the ADR.

---

49 <www.undp.org/evaluation/>

REFERENCE GROUP

The Reference Group will be formed with representatives of the Governments of the Pacific island countries, as well as representatives for civil society and private sector. The Reference Group will provide inputs to the terms of reference particularly on key evaluation questions, the inception report and the final draft of the report. To the extent possible, it will also provide feedback on the preliminary findings, conclusions and recommendations to be presented by the team in the stakeholder meeting.

The members of the Reference Group will also act as the focal points in respective Governments or organizations and will facilitate the conduct of ADR by the evaluation team by: providing necessary access to information source within each Government, and safeguarding the independence of the evaluation if required. The members will also promote the use and assist in the dissemination of the final outcomes of the ADR.

UNDP MULTI-COUNTRY OFFICES (MCOs) IN FIJI AND SAMOA, AND PACIFIC CENTRE (PC)

The MCOs/PC will support the evaluation team in liaison with key partners and other stakeholders, make available to the team all necessary information regarding UNDP's programmes, projects and activities in the countries, and provide factual verifications of the draft report. The MCOs/PC will provide the evaluation team support in kind (e.g., arranging meetings with project staff and beneficiaries; or assistance for the project site visits). To ensure the independence of the views expressed in interviews and meetings with stakeholders, however, the MCOs/PC will not participate in them.

EVALUATION TEAM

The evaluation team will be responsible for conducting the evaluation. This will entail, inter alia, establishing the evaluation plan in the inception report, conducting data collection and analysis, presenting preliminary findings, conclusions and recommendations at debriefings and the stakeholder workshop, and preparing the first, second and final drafts of the ADR report. The evaluation team will report to task manager of UNDP EO.

TRAVEL

The evaluation team may undertake field trips for interviews, group discussions, surveys and/or project site observations. The team leader will propose the travel plan in consultation with the task manager, the MCOs and other relevant stakeholders, for approval by the EO. The team leader may also be requested to travel outside Pacific, in particular to UNDP Headquarters in New York, to hold specific interviews, briefings or presentations.

TIME-FRAME

The time-frame and responsibilities for the evaluation process are detailed in Table A4.

The time-frame above is indicative of the process and deadlines, and does not imply full-time engagement of the evaluation team during the period.

EXPECTED DELIVERABLES

The expected deliverables from this exercise is the report 'Assessment of Development Results – Pacific Island Countries'.

The expected deliverables from the evaluation team in particular are:

- An inception report, providing the evaluation plan (as specified in the process section of this document).
- The first, second and final drafts of the report 'Assessment of Development Results – Pacific' (approximately 50 pages for the main text and annexes).
- Presentations at debriefings, as required, and at the stakeholder meeting.
- The final report of the ADR will follow the 'ADR Manual 2011'. All drafts will be provided in English.

Table A4. Time-Frame and Responsibilities for the Evaluation Process

Activity	Responsibility	Estimated time-frame
ADR initiation and preparatory work	EO, RBAP	Jan.-Feb. 2011
Preparatory mission	EO, MCOs	May
Selection of the evaluation team	EO	June
Preliminary research	Evaluation team	May-June
Submission of the inception report	Evaluation team	Mid-July
Data collection	Evaluation team	July-August
Data analysis	Evaluation team	September
Submission of the first draft	Evaluation team	Early October
Internal review and quality assurance	EO	October
Submission of the second draft	Evaluation team	Early November
Review by MCOs, RBAP Reference Group	RBAP, MCOs, Ref. Group	November
Stakeholder workshop	EO, MCOs RBAP, Ref. Group	End of November
Submission of the final draft	Evaluation team	Mid-December
Issuance of the final report	EO	February 2012
Dissemination of the final report	EO, RBAP, Ref. Group	First half 2012

Annex 2
EVALUATION MATRIX

CRITERIA/ SUB-CRITERIA	MAIN QUESTIONS TO BE ADDRESSED BY THE ADR	DATA SOURCES	DATA COLLECTION METHODS	(CODE)
ASSESSMENT BY THEMATIC AREA					
A.1 RELEVANCE				R
A.1a Relevance of the objectives	- Are UNDP activities aligned with national strategies? - Are they consistent with human development needs and the specific development challenges in Pacific countries?	- UNDP programme/project documents, annual work plans - Programmes/projects/thematic areas evaluation reports - National planning documents - Human development report - Interviews with beneficiaries	- Desk reviews of secondary data -Interviews with government partners - Interviews with civil society - Field visits to selected projects	(R-O)
A.1b. Relevance of approaches	- Are UNDP approaches, resources, models and conceptual frameworks realistic or relevant to achieve the planned outcomes? - Do they adhere to recognized international good practices?	- UNDP staff - Government partners involved in specific results/thematic areas - Concerned civil society partners - Development partners (UNICEF,WFP, IFAD, UNV, UN Women, bilaterals)	- Interviews with UNDP staff, development partners and government partners, civil society partners	(R-A)
A.2 EFFECTIVENESS				(E)
A.2a. Progress towards achievement of outcomes	- To what extent has the project/intervention contributed to the expected outcomes? - Has it begun a process of change that moves towards achieving the longer-term outcomes?	- Project/outcome evaluation reports - Progress reports on projects - UNDP staff - Development partners - Government partners - Beneficiaries	- Desk reviews of secondary data - Interviews with govt. partners, development partners, UNDP staff, civil society partners - Field visits to selected projects	(E-O)
A.2b. Outreach	- What is the reach (spread) of the outcomes (e.g., local community, national, regional)? - Do they reach outer island communities or areas of greatest need?	- Evaluation reports - Progress reports on projects	- Desk reviews of secondary data - Interviews with local officials	(E-OR)
A.2c. Poverty depth/equity	- Who are the main beneficiaries (poor, non-poor, disadvantaged, minorities)?	- Programme documents - Annual work plans - Evaluation reports - MDG progress reports - Human Development Reports	Desk reviews of secondary data	(E-PE)

CRITERIA/ SUB-CRITERIA	MAIN QUESTIONS TO BE ADDRESSED BY THE ADR	DATA SOURCES	DATA COLLECTION METHODS	(CODE)
A.3 EFFICIENCY				**(EF)**
A.3a Managerial efficiency	- Have programmes been implemented within deadlines and cost? - Have UNDP and its partners dealt expeditiously with implementation issues?	- Programme documents - Annual work plans - Evaluation reports - ATLAS reports - Government partners - UNDP staff (Programme Implementation Support Unit)	- Desk reviews of secondary data - Interview with government partners and UNDP staff	(EF-M)
A.3b Programmatic efficiency	- Is the programme design and management conducive to obtain the expected outcome? - Were UNDP resources focused on the set of activities that were expected to produce significant results? - Was there identified synergy between UNDP interventions that contributed to reducing costs while supporting results?	- Programme documents - Annual work plans - Evaluation reports - ATLAS reports - Government partners - Development partners - UNDP staff (Programme Implementation Support Unit)	- Desk reviews of secondary data - Interview with government partners and development partners	(EF-P)
A.4 SUSTAINABILITY				**(S)**
A.4a Design for sustainability	- Were interventions designed to have sustainable results and did they include an exit strategy?	- Programme documents - Annual work plans - Evaluation reports	- Desk reviews of secondary data - Interviews with government counterparts	(S-D)
A.4b Implementation issues: capacity development and ownership	Has national capacity been developed in the programme area to allow UNDP to realistically plan progressive disengagement? What does capacity development mean for the PICs, considering the small size of some states?	- Evaluation reports - Progress reports - UNDP programme staff	- Desk reviews of secondary data - Interviews with UNDP programme staff and govt. counterparts	(S-I)
ASSESSMENT OF UNDP STRATEGIC POSITION				
B. 1 STRATEGIC RELEVANCE AND RESPONSIVENESS				**(SRR)**
B.1a Relevance against the national development challenges and priorities	- Did UNDP address the development challenges and priorities and support the national strategies and priorities? - Did UNDP's programme facilitate the implementation of the national development strategies and policies?	- Periodic development plans of government and UNDP - Strategic documents of the UNDP, government partners, development partners - Programme documents - UNDP staff	- Interviews with UNDP staff, government partners, development partners - Desk review of secondary data	(SRR-A)
B.1b Relevance of UNDP approaches	- Is there balance between upstream and downstream initiatives? - Balance between regional/national level interventions? What is the adequacy of resources? Quality of designs, conceptual models?	- Programme portfolio - Project documents and documents outlining how projects or programmes are conceptualized and designed - Programme unit staff	- Desk review of secondary data - Interviews with programme unit staff	(SRR-L)

CRITERIA/ SUB-CRITERIA	MAIN QUESTIONS TO BE ADDRESSED BY THE ADR	DATA SOURCES	DATA COLLECTION METHODS	(CODE)
B.1c Responsiveness to changes in context	- Was UNDP responsive to the evolution over time of development challenges and the priorities in national strategies, or significant shifts due to external conditions? - Did UNDP have an adequate response to significant changes in the countries; situation, in particular in crisis and emergencies?	- UNDP staff (including management) - Other UN agencies - Government partners - Development partners	- Interviews with these informants	(SRR-C)
B.1d Balance between short-term responsiveness and long-term development objectives	- How are the short-term requests for assistance by the governments balanced against long-term development needs?	- UNDP staff (including management)	- Interviews with these informants	(SRR-SL)
B.2 ASSESSING UNDP'S USE OF NETWORKS AND COMPARATIVE STRENGTHS				**(C)**
B.2b Coordination and role sharing within the UN system, including associated funds and programmes	- Is there actual programmatic coordination with other UN agencies in the framework of UNDAF, avoiding duplications? - Did UNDP help exploit comparative advantages of associated funds (UNV, UNCDF), e.g., in specific technical matter?	- UNDP staff (including management) - Other UN agencies and funds in country - Government partners - Development partners	- Group discussion for UN system members - Interviews with government partners and development partners	(C-UFP)
B.2c Assisting governments to use partnerships and South-South cooperation	- Did UNDP use its network to bring about opportunities for South-South exchanges and cooperation?	- UNDP staff - Government partners	- Interviews with government partners	(C-PSS)
B.3 PROMOTION OF UN VALUES FROM A HUMAN DEVELOPMENT PERSPECTIVE				**(UN)**
B.3a UNDP's role in supporting policy dialogue on human development issues	- Is the UN system, and UNDP in particular, effectively engaged in policy dialogue with national actors to support development priorities? - Is the UN system, and UNDP in particular, effectively supporting the governments' monitoring of the achievement of the MDGs?	- Programme documents - Evaluation reports - HDR reports - MDG reports - National Planning Commission	- Desk review of secondary data - Interviews with government partners	(UN-HD)
B.3b Contribution to gender equality	- The extent to which the UNDP programme is designed to appropriately incorporate in each outcome area contributions to the attainment of gender equality? - The extent to which UNDP supported changes in terms of gender equality?	- Programme documents - Evaluation reports - UNDP staff - Government partners - Beneficiaries	- Desk review of secondary data - Interviews with UNDP staff and government partners - Observations from field visits	(UN-GE)
B.3c Addressing equity issues	- Did the UNDP programme take into account the plight and needs of the vulnerable or disadvantaged to promote social equity?	- Programme documents - Evaluation reports - UNDP staff - Government partners - Beneficiaries	- Desk review of secondary data - Interviews with UNDP staff and government partners - Observations from field visits	(UN-EQ)

Annex 3
SAMPLE OF PROJECTS

Thematic Area and Projects	Total Projects	Countries
Poverty Reduction and the Achievement of the MDGs	17	
Support to MDG reporting and capacity building initiatives	5	Fiji, Palau, Marshall Islands, Tonga, Vanuatu
Support to sustainable development plans	3	Kiribati, Palau, Tokelau
Support to trade policy development	2	Solomon Islands, Vanuatu
Enhance livelihood opportunities of outer island communities	2	Marshall Islands, Tuvalu
Support to entrepreneurial capacity building	1	Nauru
Support to technical cooperation among developing countries	1	Samoa
Support to aid coordination and management	2	Samoa, Solomon Islands
National Human Development Report	1	Samoa
Democratic Governance	16	
Strengthening responsive governing institutions according to Pacific Forum principles	4	Fiji, Nauru, Tokelau, Tonga
Capacity building support to parliaments and parliamentarians	4	Fiji, Niue, Palau, Samoa
Support to national initiatives on civic education	1	Fiji
Support to national elections	1	Solomon Islands
Support to E-government	1	Cook Islands
Strengthening decentralized governance	3	Kiribati, Solomon Islands, Vanuatu
Support to strengthening civil society participation	2	Tonga, Vanuatu
Environment and Sustainable Development	22	
Capacity building and mainstreaming of sustainable land management	8	Federated States of Micronesia, Fiji, Kiribati, Nauru, Niue, Marshall Islands, Samoa, Vanuatu
Promoting the sustainability of renewable energy technology	4	Fiji, Palau, Marshall Islands, Tokelau
Support to biodiversity marine conservation	3	Samoa, Tokelau, Vanuatu
Support to environment-economic governance nexus	2	Samoa, Tuvalu
Support to climate change enabling activities and national adaptation plans of action	5	Cook Is., Fiji, Kiribati, Niue, Solomon Islands
Pacific Islands ocean fishery management		Regional
Pacific Islands integrated water resource management		Regional
Pacific Islands small grants programme		Regional

Thematic Area and Projects	Total Projects	Countries
Crisis Prevention and Recovery	**5**	
Support to Tsunami early recovery	3	Samoa, Tokelau, Tonga
Support to capacity development for engendered disaster risk reduction	1	Tokelau
Strengthening capacities for peace building	1	Solomon Islands
Total projects	**60**	
Total projects by country	2	Cook Islands
	1	Federated States of Micronesia
	7	Fiji
	4	Kiribati
	3	Nauru
	3	Niue
	4	Palau
	5	Marshall Islands
	7	Samoa
	7	Solomon Islands
	5	Tokelau
	4	Tonga
	2	Tuvalu
	6	Vanuatu

Annex 4
PEOPLE CONSULTED

FEDERATED STATES OF MICRONESIA

Albert, Julita, Manager, Natural Resources, Chuuk State

Cantaro, Ricky F., Assistant Secretary, America & European Affairs

Charley, Blair, GIS Specialist, Kosrae Island Resource Management (KIRMA)

Chigiyal, Jane, Department of Foreign Affairs

Chigiyal, Mathew, Assistant Director, Division of Statistics, Office of Statistics, Budget and Economic Management, Overseas Development Assistance, and Compact Management (SBOC)

Doone, Gillian, Assistant Director, Division of Overseas Development Assistance, SBOC

Ehmes, Cindy, Assistant Director, Office of Environment and Emergency

Ehmes, Okean, Manager, Joint Presence Initiative, Pohnpei

Elymore, Jane, Department of Health and Social Welfare

Fathal, Moses, Executive, Director, Yap Community Action Programme

Fillmed, Christina, Executive Director, Environmental Protection Agency (EPA), Yap State

George, Andy, Executive Director, Kosrae Conservation and Safety Organization

Havegaichng, Frank, Director, Research and Development

Hedson, Bernolina, Secretary, Pohnpei Women's Advisory Council

Ioanis, Liwina R., Chief Clerk, Congress of FSM

Jackson, Robert, Executive Director, KIRMA

Joab, Yolonda, President, Pohnpei Youth Council

Johnson, Emihner, Island Food Community

Kostka, Willy, Director, Micronesian Conservation Trust

Maurice, Rufino, Director, National Archives, Historic and Cultural Preservation

Mikel, Ismael, Director, EPA, Chuuk State

Morgan, David, Micronesia Red Cross Society and Youth Programme Officer

Mori, Brad, Programme Manager, EPA, Chuuk State

Nakayama, W., Executive Director, Chuuk Conservation Society

Panuelo, Janet, Consultant, Social Affairs, Pohnpei State

Penno, Innocente, Director, Agriculture, Chuuk State

Shed, Patterson, Executive Director, Conservation Society of Pohnpei

Suleg, Tamoad, Chief Agricultural Officer

Susaia, Henry, Consultant, Office of Environment

PALAU

Aitaro, Gustav, Director, Bureau of International Trade and Technical Assistance

Basilius, Leonard, Coordinator, Palau Community Action Agency

Franz, Portia, Executive Officer, Environment Quality Protection Board

Kanai, Vicky, Governor, Airai State

Klouklubak, Nicholas, Energy Planner, Ministry of Public Infrastructure

Kyota, Alonzo, Director of National Emergency Management

Marion, Emma, Environment Programme Analyst, UNDP, Kadavu House, Fiji

Marino, Sebastian, National Emergency Planner, Office of Environmental Response and Coordination

Mariur, Kerai, Vice President and Minister of Finance

Ngiraingas, Madelsar, SLM Project Coordinator

Oilouch, Dennis, Director, Bureau of Budget and Planning

Temengil, Jerome, Manager, Pacific Adaptation to Climatic Change

Umetaro, Warren, Chief of Staff, Office of the Vice-President

West, Karla, Commercial Loan Officer, National Development Bank of Palau

Yano, Roman, Chief Clerk, Palau National Congress/Olbiil Era Kelulau

REPUBLIC OF MARSHAL ISLANDS

Adinimuwnu, Bernard J., Acting Secretary of Foreign Affairs

Barton, Jefferson, Director, Economic Policy, Planning and Statistics Office

Cristostomo, Yumi, Director, Office of Environmental Planning and Policy Coordination

Graham, Benjamin M., Evaluation Department, Asian Development Bank

Heine, Hilda, Advisor, Women United Together in the Marshall Islands (WUTMI)

Hess, Donald, Dr., Vice President, Academic Affairs, College of the Marshall Islands (COMI)

Hicking, Abraham, Chief, Water Quality Monitoring Lab, RMI Environmental Protection Agency

Maddison, Marie, Director, National Training Council

Momotaro, Daisy, former director, WUTMI

Momotaro, Dennis, Senator, Nitijela/Parliament

Myazoe-Debrum, Diane, Dean, Vocational and Continuing Education, COMI

Rusin, Isle, Assistant Legislative Counsel, Nitijela

Thomas, Lynna, Project Manager, Integrated Water Resource Management

Tibon, Jorelik, Deputy Chief Secretary, Office of the Chief Secretary

NAURU

GOVERNMENT

Adeang, David, Ex-Foreign Minister

Akea, Riddell, Acting Minister for Health

Ata'ata, Tai'atu, Deputy Secretary for Finance

Bautsiua, Mathew, Minister for Health, Justice and Sport

Belandres, Lolita, Consultant of Entrepreneurship Development Centre

Fritz, Creiden, Director for Commerce Industry and Environment (CIE)

Kuhu, Roland, Acting Minister for Foreign Affairs and Finance

Kun, Russ, Secretary for CIE

Lamborne, David, Secretary for Justice

Le Roy, Katy, Parliamentary Counsel

Lopiccolo, Lisa, Department of Justice

Paeniu, Seve, Secretary for Finance

Scotty, Charmaine, Secretary for Home Affairs

Tabuna, Dominic, Minister for Commerce Industry and Environment

Waqa, Barina, Department of Justice

CIVIL SOCIETY ORGANIZATIONS

Deiye, Tyron, CBOs Representative

Olsson, Julie, Nauru Islands Association of NGOs Representative

Tagamoun, Elspeth, Nauru Private Business Sector Organization

DEVELOPMENT PARTNERS

Cowled, Bruce, Australian High Commissioner

Skinner, Mark, First Secretary, AusAID

VANUATU

GOVERNMENT

National Reference Group

Kakapo, Johnny, UN Division Head/Team Leader ADR focal point, Ministry of Foreign Affairs

Tari, Peter, Deputy Governor, Reserve Bank of Vanuatu

Tavi, Collin, Monitoring and Evaluation Unit, Prime Minister's Office

Ministry of Foreign Affairs (MOFA)

Kaloris, K., MOFA

Sese, Jean, Director-General

Prime Minister's Office

Armstrong M., MDG National Coordinator

Athy, Simeon, Director-General

Naviti, Johnson, Head of Aid Coordination Unit

Nimbtik, Gregoire, Director, Department of Strategic Policy Planning and Aid Co-ordination

Reserve Bank of Vanuatu

Mathiso, Stuart, Head of Operations, National Bank of Vanuatu

Tevi, Odo, Governor, Reserve Bank of Vanuatu

Ministry of Finance and Economic Management

Maniuri, George, Director-General, Finance

Sewen, Tony, Acting Director of Finance

Ministry of Trade & Ni-Vanuatu Business

Alilee, Marokon, Director-General of Trade & Ni-Vanuatu Business

Antas, Sumbe, Director of Trade

Garae, Georgewin, Principal Cooperatives and Business Development Officer, South

Joseph, Ridley, Acting Director, Cooperatives

Joseph, Sowany, Director of Cooperatives

Rantes, Jimmy, Director of Industry

Williams, Timothy, Principal Trade Officer, IF Focal Point

Wotu, Ben, Director of Customs

Ministry of Internal Affairs

Ala, Cherol, Director of Department of Local Authorities

Bogiri, George, Director-General

Kaltamat, Edward, Deputy Director of Department of Local Authorities

Tabi, Ben, Principal Development Planning Officer

Ministry of Lands

Dick, Richard, Director of Lands

Galileo, William, SLM, Project Coordinator

Williams, Albert, Director of Environment Department/GEF Focal Point

Meteorology

Philips, Brian, Chairman of National Advisory Committee on Climate Change and National Coordinator

Public Works Department

Alpones, Dennis, Pacific Adaptation to Climate Change (PACC) Project Coordinator

Watson, Willie, PACC Project Coordinator

Ministry of Education

Joe, Jessie Dick, Director-General

Niroa, John, Director, Policy and Planning

Obed, Director, Education Services

Ministry of Agriculture, Forestry and Fisheries

Markwood, Ruben Bakeo, Director of Agriculture

Mele, Livo, Director of Forestry

Tate, Hanington, Acting Director

Wilfred, Jeffery, Director-General of Agriculture

CIVIL SOCIETY ORGANIZATIONS

Kalotap, Mark, Live & Learn

Kalsuak, Ian, World Vision

Licht, Viviane, CEO, Vanuatu Association of NGO

Molisa, Sela, Member of Parliament – Chairman of Steering Committee for High Level Conference on Global Economic Conference

Nimoho, Leah, GEF/SGP, National Coordinator

Peter, Josephine, SPC, Regional Rights Resource Team Focal Point

Solomon, Kathy, Director, VDRTCA

Soulier, Christine, Vanuatu Rural Development and Training Centres Association

Wallez, Andrine, ACTIV ASSOCIATION

Vanuatu Transparency International

Bryard, Francis, Senior Project Coordinator

Patterson, Marie Noel, Head

Vanuatu Chamber of Commerce

Kalnpel, Louis, General Manager

Massing, Joe, Advocacy Officer

Vanwods, John Salong, General Manager

DEVELOPMENT PARTNERS

AusAID Programme Office in Vanuatu

Brien, Derek, Executive Director, Pacific Institute of Public Policy (PIPP)

Chen Li, Chinese Embassy, First Secretary, Economic and Commercial Counsellor's Office

David, Roselyne Arthur, UN Affairs Officer/Country Development Manager

European Union Team

Falemaka, Merawalesi, Director, Trade and Investment Division

French Embassy

McNaughton, Belynda, First Secretary (Health and Education), NZ High Commission

Nirua, Jean Pierre, Melanesian Spearhead Group (MSG), Head-Acting Director-General

Pascual, May Susan, Chief of UNICEF Vanuatu Field Office and UN Joint Presence

Ruiz-Avila, Katherine, Officer of the Australian Government's overseas aid programme AusAID

Sikivou, Peni, Director, Economic and Social Development Division

World Bank/ADB Office

Wouloseje, Donald, UNDP Programme Officer

KIRIBATI

GOVERNMENT

Ministry of Environment, Lands and Agricultural Development (MELAD)

Anchita, PPU, MELAD

Reiher, Taouea, OIC, Environment and Conservation Division (ECD)

Soa, Tianeti, Agriculture

Tabutoa, Ruui, Assistant Secretary

Tebutonga, Director of Lands

Tooma, Wiriki, Secretary, MELAD

Toto, Kaateti, Senior Assistant Secretary

Vaimalie, Rateiti, SLM Coordinator

Ministry of Foreign Affairs and Immigration

Kautu, Anne, Senior Women Development Officer

Komono, Depweh, Secretary

Wilson, Mauea, Senior Youth Development Officer

Ministry of Finance and Economic Development

Erekana, Tiare, OIC, Ministry of Commerce, Industry and Cooperatives (MCIC),

Koina, Boorau, Project Accountant and Administrator

Mika, Saitofi, Economist

Robuti, Kurinati, Senior Economist

Secretary, Ministry of Internal and Social Affairs

Secretary, MCIC

CIVIL SOCIETY ORGANIZATIONS

Komeri, Onerio

Small Grants Community Projects

Tiantet, CEO, Kiribati Solar Energy Company

Tokitebwa, T., Utility Manager

DEVELOPMENT PARTNERS

AusAID

Erikate, Kakiateiti

Kaiwai, Robert, Ambassador, New Zealand Embassy, Tarawa

Milligan, Aimee

UNDP

Momoe Kham

Nuzhat & Aren

TONGA

Anisi, Onetoto, Project Office, MDG, Ministry of Finance and National Planning

Bing, Rosomond, Legal Administrator, Ministry of Land, Survey and Natural Resources (MLSNR)

Blake, Betty, Civil Society Forum of Tonga (CSFT)

Blake, Vake, National Women's Council (NWC)

Fakaosi, Lopeti, CSFT

Faletau, Tufui, Policy and Planning Division, MOFNP

Fifita, Luisi, Community Town Officer, Kolavai Village

Fotu, Salesi, Acting Secretary, MLSNR

Ilohahia, Siale, Director, CSFT

Kalaniuvalu, Uboina, NWC

Mafi, Lucy, Country Officer, UNESCO

Ma'u, Paula, CEO, Ministry of Information and Communication

Paunga, Polotu, Director, Women's Affairs Unit, Ministry of Education, Women and Culture

Pohia, Siosiua P'ol, CSFT

Pouvalu, Emily, Director, Ministry of Culture

Soakai, Alfred, Deputy Secretary, Prime Minister's Office

Takai, Maliu, Project Manager, Ministry of Finance and National Planning

Totuu, Luisa, Senior Officer, Ministry of Education, Women and Culture

Tuita, Milika, Programme Analyst, UNDP

Tupyniua, Maheuliuli nSandhurst, CEO/Secretary, Foreign Affairs

Vi, Hauoli, NWC

Vuki, Pikts, Commissioner and Supervisor, Electoral Office

COOK ISLANDS

Carruthers, Pashia, Manager, Island Futures Division, National Environment Service (NES)

Edgar, Jane, Delegate, International Federation of Red Cross and Red Crescent Societies

Epati, Navy, Commissioner, Public Sector Commission (PSC)

Malcom, Roger, Former Mayor, Aitutaki and consultant, Outer Islands Development Programme (OIDP)

Maruariki, Priscilla, CEO, PSC

Mataroa, Keu, National PACC Focal Point, Ministry of Infrastructure and Planning

Mataroa, Vaipo, National Coordinator, PACC

Rattle, Niki, Secretary General, Red Cross

Samuel, Reboama, Disaster Risk Reduction Coordinator

Tangianau, Otheniel, former project manager, OIDP

Teurata, Tania, Deputy Director, NES

Tupa, Vaitoti, Director, NES

Unuia, Tou (Man), Outer Island Project Coordinator

Wichman, Vaine, former consultant to UNDP

Wright-Koteka, Elizabeth, Director, Central Planning and Policy, Office of Prime Minister

NIUE

Makola, Grizelda, former Youth Parliamentarian, Ministry of Health

Talagi, Haden, Coordinator of PACC in Niue, Ministry of Environment

Tongahai, Bortha, former project officer, Youth Parliament, Ministry of Education

Tukiuha, President, Organic Farmers Association

TUVALU

Hoamsi, Annie, Coordinator and Executive Director, Tuvalu Association of Non-Governmental Organizations

Ito, Assistant Representative, Japan International Cooperation Agency (JICA)

Laafai, Puisneli, Principal Secretary for FATTEL, Ministry of Home Affairs and Rural Development

Matsudate, Fumiko, project coordinator, JICA

Matsui, Noaki, Adviser to PM, JICA

Miamaki, University of Tokyo

Samasoni, Lopati, project manager, Support to Local Governance Project

Tamura, Minoru, project manager, Project Formulation Advisor, JICA

Taupo, Minute, Permanent Secretary, Ministry of Finance and Planning

Taupo, Susana, Project Coordinator, Sustainable Land Management

Toafa, Pula, Director, National Council of Women

TOKELAU

GOVERNMENT

Puka-Mauga, Ake, Tokelau Office in Apia

Suveinakama, Jovelisi, Tokelau Office in Apia

DEVELOPMENT PARTNERS

UNDP

Bonin, Georgina, Assistant Resident Representative, UNDP Samoa Multi-Country Office (MCO)

Noble, Nileema, Resident Representative, UNDP Samoa MCO

FIJI

GOVERNMENT

Bebeia, Tari, Economic Planning Officer, Ministry of Strategic Planning

Boelawa, Eliki, Advisor, Reserve Bank of Fiji

Prasad, Krishna, Ministry of Strategic Planning

Quregave, Aminiasi, Secretary, Local Government, Urban Development, Housing and Environment (LGUDHE)

Raiwalui, Anare, Principal Fisheries Officer (Oceanic), Fisheries Department

Tagivuni, Sele, LGUDHE

Turaganwalu, Marcia, Senior Economic Planning Officer, Ministry of Finance

Walker, Ernst, Chief Economic Planning Officer, Strategic Planning Office

CIVIL SOCIETY ORGANIZATIONS

Ali, Muhammad Shamim, Executive Education Office, Fiji Muslim League

Costello-Olsson, Koila, Director, Pacific Centre for Peace Building

Evening, Susane, Catholic Women's League

Kini, Isikeli, Methodist Church

Prakash, Vijendra, Sanatan Fiji

Rolls, Sharon Bhagwan, Executive Director, FemLink Pacific

Swamy, William, National Vice President, FemLink Pacific

Venkataiya, Sheela, Education Director, T.I.S.I. Sangam

Vereti, Laisa, Programme Officer, Pacific Islands Association of Non-Governmental Organizations

Vilsoni, Sumasafu, Fiji Disabled Peoples Federation

REGIONAL ORGANIZATIONS

Holland, Paula, Manager Naturak Resources Governance, SOPAC Division, Secretariat of the Pacific Community (SPC)

Nimmo, Rick, Director Political Governance and Security Programme, Pacific Islands Forum

Utoikamanu, Fekitamoeloa K., Deputy Director-General, Suva Regional Office, SPC

Webb, Arthur, Deputy Director, Ocean and Islands Programme, SPC

DONORS

Dirks, Richard, First Secretary (Bilateral Development), New Zealand High Commission

Goundar, Nilesh, Programme Manager (UN Partnerships and Gender), Australian High Commission

Kwesius, Romaine, Counselor, Development Cooperation Division, Australian High Commission

Ramsey, Fiona, Second Secretary (Social Sectors), European Union

UN SYSTEM

Abrioux, Emmanuelle, Chief of Education, UNICEF

Ahn, I., Representative, WHO

Bogner, Matida, Regional Adviser, OHCHR

Cocco-Klein, Samantha, Chief Policy, Advocacy, Planning and Evaluation, UNICEF

Jena, Dirk, Director and Representative, UNFPA

Kanervavuori, Mika, Human Rights Officer, OHCHR

Lamotte, David, Representative, ILO

Lindberg, Lena, Regional Programme Director (OIC), UNWOMEN

Molendijk, Simon Jan, Child Friendly School Specialist, UNICEF

Muller, Peter, Regioanl Disaster Response Advisor, OCHA

Naduva, Adriu, Programme Specialist, UNFPA

Ndombi, Isiye, Representative, UNICEF

Planitz, Angelika, Subregional Coordinator, Pacific, UNISDR

Rwabuhemba, Tim, Regional Coordinator, UNAIDS

UNDP

Bower, Mereseini, team leader, Poverty Reduction and MDGs

Hussain, Naheed, team leader, Programme Support Unit

Kurbanov, Toily, Deputy Resident Representative

Liew, Jeff, Regional Financial Capacity Adviser, Pacific Financial Inclusion Programme

Nabou, Sainimili, team leader, Governance

Mario, Emma, Environment OIC

Moustafa, Ahmed, MDGs and Poverty Reduction Team Leader, Pacific Centre

Ostby, Knut, Resident Coordinator and Resident Representative

Ravuvu, Asenaca, Assistant Resident Representative (Programme)

Rodrigues, Charmaine, Regional Governance Specialist, Pacific Centre

Wiseman, Garry, Manager, Pacific Centre

SAMOA

Fau, Tamati, Climate Change and Health Coordinator, National Health Service

Faumui, Aida, ACEO, Trade Division, Ministry of Foreign Affairs and Trade (MFAT)

Fong, Peseta Frank, ACEO, Ministry Of Agriculture and Fisheries

Galuvao-Motalavea, Leilani, Information and Communication Specialist, Ministry of Health

Imo, Foketi, DCEO, Operations Management Department, Ministry of Finance

Liuga, Faumuina Tiatia Faaolatane, Minister for Finance

Matulino, Jacinta Malie, Senior Industry Development and Investment Promotion Office, Ministry of Commerce, Industry and Labour

Momoemausa, Melama, National Project Coordinator, Division of Environment and Conservation, Ministry of Natural Resources and Environment (MNRE)

Paniani, Taputo ACEO, Forestry Division, MNRE

Simi, Noumea, DCEO Aid, Ministry of Finance

Siova, Ullesi, ACEO, Health Promotion and Preventive Services

So'o, Asofea, Vice-Chancellor, National University of Samoa

Tanupopo, Henry, Principal Foreign Service Officer, MFAT

CIVIL SOCIETY ORGANIZATIONS

High Chief Vaasiliifiti Moelagi Jackson, National President, Samoa Umbrella for Non-Governmental Organizations (SUNGO)

Voigt, Raymond C., National Treasurer, SUNGO

UNDP

Alexis, Armstrong, Coordinator Programme and Operations

Bonin, Georgina, Assistant Resident Representative (Programme)

Stegemann, Judith, Intern

SOLOMON ISLANDS

GOVERNMENT

Ata, Fr. Sam, Chair, Truth and Reconciliation Commission (TRC)

Daonga, Allan, Under Secretary, Ministry of Development Planning and Aid Coordination (MDPAC)

Iroi, Chanel, Under Secretary, Ministry of Environment, Climate Change, and Disaster Management (MECDM)

Kemakeza, Sir Allen, Speaker of National Parliament

Kere, Joy, Permanent Secretary, Ministry of National Unity, Reconciliation and Peace

Kusilifu, Dvaid, Director, Committees

Legua, Nancy, Under Secretary, Ministry of Provincial Governance and Institutional Strengthening (MPGIS)

Macher, Sofia, Commissioner, TRC

Nesol, Florence, Deputy Clerk, National Parliament

Rukale, Lennis, Permanent Secretary, MPGIS

Sanga, Taeasi, Clerk, National Parliament

Sisilo, Robert, Permanent Secretary, Ministry of Foreign Affairs and External Trade (MFAET)

Sore, Rene, Permanent Secretary, MECDM

Walegerea, Cornelius, Director (Acting), Aid Coordination Unit, MDPAC

Wara, Samuel, Chief Planning Officer, MDPAC

Yates, Loti, Director, National Disaster Management Office

DONORS

Hinojosa, Juan Carlos, Attaché-Social Sectors/Governance, European Union

Obata, Hitomi, Researcher/Advisor, Embassy of Japan

Representative, AusAID, Honiara

Representative, Regional Assistance Mission to Solomon Islands, Honiara

Wong, Sarah, Development Counsellor, New Zealand High Commission, Honiara

CIVIL SOCIETY ORGANIZATIONS

Hadosaia, Clement, Manager, Kastor Garden Associates

Lado, Shepherd, Acting Executive Officer, Transparency Solomon Islands

Ruqebatu, Collin, General Secretary, Development Services Exchange

Teakeni, Josephine, Director, Vois Blong Mere Solomon

Wate, Jennifer, Director, Solomon Island Development Trust

UNDP

Devesi, Jude, Assistant Resident Representative

Suzaki, Akiko, Deputy Resident Representative

Annex 5
DOCUMENTS CONSULTED

Abbott, D., 'Poverty in the Pacific: Definitions, Trends and Issues', A Slide Presentation from the Regional Macroeconomic and Poverty Reduction Advisor, UNDP Subregional Centre, Suva, Fiji, unpublished document.

Abbott, D. and S. Pollard, 'Hardship and Poverty in the Pacific', Asian Development Bank, Manila, 2004.

Asian Development Bank, 'A Different Kind of Voyage, Development and Dependence in the Pacific Islands', Manila, 1998.

Asian Development Bank, 'A Pacific Strategy for the New Millennium', Manila, September 2000.

Asian Development Bank, 'Asian Development Outlook, 2010', Manila, 2010.

Asian Development Bank, 'Cook Islands 2001 Economic Report: Policies for Progress' Manila, December 2002.

Asian Development Bank, 'Governance in the Pacific: Focus for Action 2005-09', Manila, 2004.

Asian Development Bank, 'Improving Growth Prospects in the Pacific', Manila, March 1998.

Asian Development Bank, 'Marshall Islands: 2000-Economic Report and Statement of Development Strategies', Manila, April 2001.

Asian Development Bank, 'Poverty: Is It An Issue in the Pacific?', Manila, March 2001.

Asian Development Bank, 'Pursuing Economic Reform in the Pacific', Manila, October 1999.

Asian Development Bank, 'Reforms in the Pacific: An Assessment of ADB's Assistance for Reform Programmes in the Pacific', Manila, October 1999.

Asian Development Bank, 'Republic of the Fiji Islands 1999 Economic Report', Manila, April 2000.

Asian Development Bank, 'Responding to the Priorities of the Poor: A Pacific Strategy for the Asian Development Bank 2005-09', Manila, 2004.

Asian Development Bank, 'RETA 6065, Assessing Community Perspectives on Governance in the Pacific', Manila, 2002

Asian Development Bank, 'Samoa 2000: Building on Recent Reforms', Manila, November 2000.

Asian Development Bank, 'Solomon Islands: 1997 Economic Report', Manila, August 1998.

Asian Development Bank, 'The Millennium Development Goals in Pacific Island Countries: Taking Stock, Emerging Issues, and the Way Forward', Manila, 2004.

Asian Development Bank, 'Tonga: Natural Resources Use and Sustainable Socioeconomic Development', April 2002.

Asian Development Bank, 'Tuna: A Key Economic Resource in the Pacific Islands', Manila, April 2001.

Asian Development Bank, 'Tuvalu: 2002 Economic and Public Sector Review', Manila, November 2002.

Asian Development Bank, 'Vanuatu: Economic Performance and Challenges Ahead', Manila, April 2002.

Asian Development Bank, 'Vanuatu: Policy Issues in the Agriculture, Fisheries, and Forestry Sectors', Manila, May 2002.

AusAID, 'Pacific 2020: Challenges and Opportunities for Growth', Canberra, 2006.

AusAID, 'Violence Against Women in Melanesia and East Timor: Building on Global and Regional Promising Approaches', Department of Development Effectiveness, Canberra, 2008

Bolger, J., 'Pacific Choice: Learning from Success', Asian Development Bank, Manila, 2008.

Crocombe, R., *The South Pacific*, The University of the South Pacific, Suva, 2001.

Duncan, R., and Hakagawa, H., 'Obstacles to Economic Growth in Six Pacific Island Countries,' Working Paper, World Bank, Washington DC, 2007.

Firth, R., *History and Traditions of Tikopia*, Polynesian Society, Wellington, 1961.

Freedom House, 'Freedom in the World 2011: The authoritarian challenge to democracy', available at <www.freedomhouse.org/images/File/fiw/FIW_2011_Booklet.pdf>

GEF, 'National Capacity Needs Assessment for Global Environment Management', Project Document (PIMS 2549), 2004.

GEF, 'Request for CEO Endorsement/Approval for a Medium Size Project', Project Request Document (PIMS 3093), 2007.

Gegeo, D., 'Kastom and bisnis: Towards integrating cultural knowledge into rural development in the Solomon Islands', Ph.D. dissertation. University of Hawaii, Honolulu, 1994.

Government of the Federated States of Micronesia (FSM), 'Millennium Development Goals & The Federated States of Micronesia: Status Report', FSM Government Publications, Pohnpei, 2010.

Government of FSM/UNDP, 'Capacity Building for Sustainable Management in FSM: A Mid Term Review' by K. Englberger and O. Wortel, Pohnpei, June 2011.

Government of FSM/UNDP, 'Country Programme Action Plan (CPAP) for FSM', 2008-2012.

Government of FSM/UNDP, 'Preparatory Assistance Project on the Strengthening of the FSM Congress and State Legislatures', Project Document, January-December 2008.

Government of FSM/UNDP and GEF, 'Capacity Building, Capacity Development, and Mainstreaming of Sustainable Land Development', Project Document, 2008-2012.

Gregory, A., 'Tokelau Votes to Remain Dependent Territory of New Zealand', *New Zealand Herald*, 25 October 2007.

Hazel, F.X., *The New Shape of Old Cultures: A Half Century of Social Change in Micronesia*, University of Hawaii Press, Honolulu, 2001.

House, W.J., 'The Role and Significance of Population Policies in the Pacific Islands', *Pacific Health Dialog*, Vol. 2. No. 1, Suva, 1995.

Howard, A., *Learning to be a Rotuman*, Columbia Teachers College Press, New York, 1966.

International Fund for Agricultural Development, 'The Global Mechanism: United Nations Convention to Combat Desertification. Climate Change Impacts – Pacific Islands', available at <www.ifad.org/events/apr09/impact/islands.pdf>.

Jivan, V. and Forster, C. 'Translating CEDAW Into Law: CEDAW Legislative Compliance in Nine Pacific Island Countries', UNDP Pacific Centre and UNIFEM Pacific Regional Office, Suva, 2006.

Least Developed Countries Website available at <www.ldcgroups.org>.

Maud, H.E., *The Gilbertese Maneaba*, The University of the South Pacific, Suva, 1980.

Meleisea, P.S. and Meleisea, E. 'The Elimination of All Forms of Discrimination and Violence against the Girl Child: Situation Paper for the Pacific Island Region', prepared for UNIFEM and UNICEF, 2003

Nabobo-Baba, U., *Knowing and Learning: An Indigenous Fijian Approach*, The University of the South Pacific, Suva, 2006.

NGO Working Group on Women, Peace and Security, 'A Call to Ensure Women's Participation in Resolving the Conflict in the Solomon Islands', Press Release, New York, 12 May 2006.

Pacific Islands Forum Secretariat, '2010 Pacific Regional MDGs Tracking Report', Suva, July 2010.

Pacific Islands Forum Secretariat, 'The Pacific Plan for Strengthening Regional Cooperation and Integration', Suva, 2007.

Rasanathan, J.J.K. and Bhushan, A. 'Measuring and Responding to Gender-based Violence in the Pacific: Action on Gender Inequality as a Social Determinant of Health', Republic of Kiribati, WHO Regional Office for the Western Pacific, October 2011,

Ravuvu, A., *The Fijian Ethos*, The University of the South Pacific, Suva, 1987.

Republic of Marshall Islands (RMI)/UNDP, 'Action for the Development of Marshall Islands Renewal Energies (ADMIRE)', Project Document (PIMS#3094), 2008.

RMI/UNDP, 'Annual Activity Report for RMI for 2009'.

RMI/UNDP, 'Capacity Building for Sustainable Management in the Marshall Islands', Project Document, 2008.

RMI/UNDP, 'Evaluation of the UNDP Republic of the Marshall Islands Support to Parliament Project: Final Report', by Prof Nakamura and Ms Charmaine Rodrigues, 2007.

RMI/UNDP, 'Marshall Islands Support to Nitijela (Parliament) Project Phase Two', Project Document.

RMI/UNDP, 'Minutes of the RMI Sustainable Livelihood Development Project Tripartite Review Meeting', by Patrick Tuimaleai'ifano, 4 September 2006.

RMI/UNDP, 'Minutes of the RMI Sustainable Livelihood Development Project Tripartite Review Meeting', by Patrick Tuimaleai'ifano, December 2007.

RMI/UNDP, 'Multi-Country Programme Outcomes/Indicators', 2004.

Republic of Palau (ROP), 'National Capacity for Self-Assessment: Final Report', 2006.

ROP/GEF, 'Sustainable Economic Development Through Renewal Energy Applications (SEDREA) Project', Project Document, (PIMS 3093), 2008.

ROP/UNDP, 'Annual Project Report on the Support to Palau Congress Project', 2010.

ROP/UNDP, 'Capacity Building for Sustainable Land Management for Mitigation of Land Degradation (SLM)', Project Document (PIMS 3401), 2008.

ROP/UNDP, 'Country Programme Action Plan (CPAP) 2008-2012', 2008.

ROP/UNDP, 'Preparatory Assistance Project on the Strengthening of the Palau Olbiil Era Kelulau (Legislature)', Project Document, 2008.

ROP/UNDP, 'Republic of Palau UNDAT Joint Programme Outcomes', 2010.

Sahlins, M., *Moala: Culture and Nature on a Fijian Island*, University of Michigan Press, Ann Arbor, 1962.

Stahl, Charles W. and Appleyard, Reginald T., 'Migration in the Pacific Islands: Lessons from the New Zealand Experience', Australian Agency for International Development, Canberra, April 2007.

Tokelau Government, 'Tokelau National Strategic Plan'.

UNDP, 'Fiji Country Programme Action Plan (2008-2012)'.

UNDP, 'Human Development Report 2011', Available at <hdr.undp.org/en/>.

UNDP, 'Kiribati Country Programme Action Plan (CPAP) 2008-2012'.

UNDP, 'Kiribati MDG Report 2007'

UNDP, 'Multi-Country Programme Document 2003-2007'.

UNDP, 'Multi-Country Programme Document 2008-2012'.

UNDP, 'Pacific Project Implementation Reviews, SLM Project', 2009.

UNDP, 'Palau Annual Performance Report, SLM Project', 2011.

UNDP, 'Samoa Country Programme Action Plan (2008-2012)'.

UNDP, 'Solomon Island, Country Programme Action Plan (2008-2012)'.

UNDP, 'Tokelau Country Programme Action Plan 2008-2012'.

UNDP, 'Tonga MDG Assessment Survey 2010'.

UNDP, 'UNDP Pacific Centre Annual Report 2010: Connecting with Partners for Transformational Change in the Pacific', Suva, 2010.

UNDP, 'Vanuatu Country Programme Action Plan (CPAP) 2008-2012'

UNDP, 'Vanuatu MDG Report 2010'

UNDP Multi-Country Office, Fiji, 'Environment and Sustainable Management: Country Development Managers Workshop', Suva, 12 August 2008.

UNDP Multi-Country Office, Fiji, Website: <undp.org.fj>

UNDP Multi-Country Office, Samoa, Website: <undp.org.ws>

UNDP and Government of Fiji, 'Final Evaluation of the National Initiative on Civic Education (NICE) Project', Suva, April 2011.

UNDP and UNFPA, 'Multi-Country Programme Document, 2008-2012: Federated States of Micronesia, Fiji, Kiribati, Marshall Islands, Nauru, Palau, Solomon Islands, Tonga, Tuvalu and Vanuatu', New York, 2007.

UNEP, 'Pacific Islands Environment Outlook 1999', Nairobi, 1999.

UNFCCC, 'Vulnerability and Adaptation to Climate Change in Small Island Developing States', Secretariat of the United Nations Framework Convention on Climate Change, Bonn, 2005.

United Nations, 'Common Country Assessment: Desk Review: Federated States of Micronesia', 2011.

United Nations, Department of Economic and Social Affairs. Population Division. Population Estimates and Projections Section Website available at <www.un.org/esa/population/>.

United Nations, 'Pacific Sub-Region United Nations Development Assistance Framework (UNDAF) (2008-2012)', Mid Term Review, May-July 2010.

United Nations, 'Sustainable Development in the Pacific', Economic and Social Commission for Asia and the Pacific, Subregional Office for the Pacific, Suva, April 2010, Available at <www.sidsnet.org/msi_5/docs/regional/pacific/Pacific_Regional_Synthesis-MSI5-Final.pdf>.

United States Government Census Bureau Webpage available at <www.census.gov>.

World Bank, 'Evaluation of World Bank Assistance to Pacific Members Countries, 1992-2002'. Operations Evaluation Department, Washington DC, March 2005.

World Bank, 'Expanding Job Opportunities for Pacific Islanders through Labor Mobility at Home and Away', Washington, DC, 2006.